WWW

By the same author
and published by Rationality Publications

When Time Is at a Premium: Cognitive-Behavioural Approaches to Single-Session Therapy and Very Brief Coaching (2016)

Attitudes in Rational Emotive Behaviour Therapy (REBT): Components, Characteristics and Adversity-Related Consequences (2016)

Windy Dryden Live! (2021)

Windy Dryden Collected! (2022)

The REBT Pocket Companion for Clients, 2nd Edition (with Walter J. Matweychuk) (2022)

The Little Book of Therapeutic Rationality (2022)

Thought for the Day: A Flexible Approach to Mental Health (2022)

Seizing Moments and Being Useful: The Development of a Single-Session Therapist (2025)

'Seven Principles' Series

Seven Principles of Good Mental Health (2021)

Seven Principles of Rational Emotive Behaviour Therapy (2021)

Seven Principles of Single-Session Therapy (2021)

Seven Principles of Doing Live Therapy Demonstrations (2021)

WWW

The Collected Wonderful Words of Windy

Windy Dryden

Rationality Publications

Rationality Publications
136 Montagu Mansions, London W1U 6LQ

www.rationalitypublications.com
info@rationalitypublications.com

This edition published by Rationality Publications
Copyright (c) 2025 Windy Dryden

A catalogue record of this book is
available from the British Library.

First edition 2025

ISBN: 978-1-914938-41-2

Contents

Preface 7
Acknowledgements 8

1. On the *ABC* Framework 9
2. On Rigid and Flexible Attitudes 12
3. On Unbearability and Bearability Attitudes 23
4. On Awfulising and Non-awfulising Attitudes 27
5. On Devaluation and Acceptance Attitudes 30
6. On Psychological Disturbance 39
7. On Anxiety 43
8. On Depression 51
9. On Shame 58
10. On Guilt 63
11. On Regret 68
12. On Anger 72
13. On Hurt 79
14. On Jealousy 83
15. On Envy 88
16. On Avoidance and Withdrawal 93
17. On Failure 94
18. On Perfectionism 95
19. On Uncertainty and Making Decisions 97
20. On Procrastination 100
21. On Self-Discipline 103
22. On Responsibility and Control 106
23. On Relationships with Others 108
24. On Assertion 115
25. On Parents 117
26. On Being Human 119
27. On Critical Thinking 121
28. On Personal Change 124
29. On Good Mental Health 139
30. Miscellaneous 145
31. 'Little Gems' from Therapy Demonstrations 150

Postscript 156
Index 157

Preface

I have long been interested in the use of aphorisms, maxims and sayings in therapy and coaching. They tend to be brief, vivid and contain useful observations for how to improve one's mental health and promote personal development. Over the years, I have compiled a list of my own statements and have published a number of such volumes (Dryden, 1999, 2022a, 2022b). In addition, I have published a book of brief advice to clients engaged in Rational Emotive Behaviour Therapy to help them understand this therapy and how to get the most from it (Dryden, 2003; Dryden & Matweychuk, 2022).

As I approach the end of my career, I have decided to bring together some of my work in collected form (e.g., Dryden, 2022c). The present volume is a collection of my own 'wise words' and encapsulations of REBT drawn from the publications mentioned above. It also contains, for the first time, a number of 'little gems' I said during therapy demonstrations with volunteers (Dryden, 2021) and designed to help them deal with their nominated issues in ways that might be considered memorable. In addition to being comprehensive, this book is more logically organised than my previous publications in this genre and is divided into thirty-one parts.

References

Dryden, W. (1999). *A Positive Thought for Every Day*. Sheldon.

Dryden, W. (2003) *The REBT Pocket Companion for Clients*. Albert Ellis Institute.

Dryden, W. (2021). *Seven Principles of Doing Live Therapy Demonstrations*. Rationality Publications.

Dryden, W. (2022a). *The Little Book of Therapeutic Rationality*. Rationality Publications.

Dryden, W. (2022b). *Thought for the Day: A Flexible Approach to Mental Health*. Rationality Publications.

Dryden, W. (2022). *Windy Dryden Collected!* Rationality Publications.

Dryden, W., and Matweychuk, W. (2022). *The REBT Pocket Companion for Clients. 2nd edition.* Rationality Publications.

Note

Items that are linked are shown by a connected downward arrow in the middle of the page.

Acknowledgements

This book could not have been written without the contribution of many REBT therapists I have known since 1978. In this regard, I wish to mention my good friend and colleague, Dr. Walter Matweychuk who has consistently flown the REBT flag even when times were tough for him. Special thanks go to Georgie Aronin, who has transcribed over 800 of my therapy demonstrations and who coined the term 'little gems' for the memorable statements I made to volunteers in these demonstrations. She also suggested what should be regarded as 'little gems'.

1

On the *ABC* Framework

1. In this book, I will use the *ABC* framework used by myself and my colleagues who practise Rational Emotive Behaviour Therapy:

> *A* = *A*dversity
> *B* = *B*asic Attitudes (held toward the adversity)
> - Rigid and extreme attitudes
> - Flexible and non-extreme attitudes
> *C* = *C*onsequences of holding these attitudes towards A
> - Emotional consequences
> - Behavioural consequences
> - Thinking consequences

2. The world is where things happen to us. The brain is where we process this stuff.
    So, World x Brain = Response

3. Epictetus, the famous Roman philosopher, said that men are disturbed not by things, but by their view of things. The REBT version of this is as follows: 'People are not disturbed by things. Rather, they make themselves disturbed about things by the rigid and extreme attitudes that they take towards these things.'

4. Unhealthy basic attitudes at *B* which are the prime targets of change in the *ABC* framework have the following characteristics:

    a. They are rigid and extreme.
    b. They largely lead to dysfunctional emotive, behavioural, and thinking consequences.
    c. They are inconsistent with reality.
    d. They are illogical and nonsensical.

e. They largely impede you as you pursue your healthy goals.

f. They largely interfere with your productive work and interpersonal relationships.

5. REBT outlines four major rigid and extreme attitudes:

a. **Rigid attitudes** (e.g., musts, oughts, absolute shoulds, got to's)

b. **Unbearability attitudes** (e.g., 'It is unbearable'; 'I can't stand it'; 'It's intolerable')

c. **Awfulising attitudes** (e.g., 'It's terrible that...'; 'It's awful that...'; 'It's the end of the world that...')

d. **Devaluation attitudes** (e.g., 'I'm no good'; 'You're no good'; 'Life is no good').

6. REBT's *ABC* model of psychological disturbance stresses the central role that rigid and extreme attitudes play in determining psychological disturbance. In doing this, REBT does not imply that adversities at *A* play an unimportant role in your problems. Such adversities contribute significantly to your disturbance, even though they do not determine it.

7. You may think that severe adversities, such as being raped or having a loved one murdered, cause psychological disturbance. While this is understandable, it is again wide of the mark. Such atrocities do cause great distress, but distress is based on flexible and non-extreme thinking. Disturbance differs from distress because it is based on rigid and extreme thinking. So, the goal of REBT in these cases is to help you to work through your great distress about severe adversities while freeing yourself from the interfering presence of disturbance.

8. Healthy attitudes at *B* in the *ABC* framework have the following characteristics:

    a. They are flexible and non-extreme.

    b. They largely lead to functional emotive, behavioural and thinking consequences.

    c. They are consistent with reality.

    d. They are logical and make sense.

    e. They largely help you as you pursue your healthy goals.

    f. They largely sustain and improve your productive work and interpersonal relationships.

9. REBT outlines four major healthy attitudes:

    a. **Flexible attitudes** – in which you acknowledge what you want, but you actively assert that you do not absolutely have to get what you want.

    b. **Bearability attitudes** – in which you acknowledge that it is a struggle putting up with not getting your desires met, facing certain difficult circumstances, or the inner tension that is experienced under aversive conditions. However, you actively assert that you can bear this, recognise that it is well worth bearing, that you are worth bearing it for, that you are willing to bear the struggle, and that you commit to doing so.

    c. **Non-awfulising attitudes** – in which you acknowledge it is bad when you don't get what you want, but you actively assert that it isn't the end of the world, you can transcend not getting it, and good can come from bad.

    d. **Unconditional acceptance attitudes** – in which you acknowledge that both you and others are complex, unratable, unique, fallible human beings who are constantly in flux. You also acknowledge that life is incredibly rich and complex and can definitely not be given a single fixed, global rating.

2

On Rigid and Flexible Attitudes

10. Rigid and extreme attitudes underpin a psychologically disturbed response to adversity.

11. **Rigid attitudes** (musts, absolute shoulds, got to's) are unhealthy for the following reasons:

   a. **They generally yield poor results:**
   While a rigid attitude may have some positive results (e.g., it may be motivating), by and large, most of the results it yields are poor (e.g., it results in anxiety; thus, its motivating effect is contaminated by anxiety and with the inefficiency that often goes with it).

   b. **They are false:**
   If there were a law of the universe that states you absolutely must do well, then you could not fail to do well. It would be impossible for you to fail. This is obviously untrue.

   c. **They are illogical:**
   A rigid attitude comprises two components – a non-rigid component (e.g., 'I want to do well') and a rigid component ('…therefore I must do well'). The latter does not logically follow from the former, since you logically cannot derive something rigid from something that is non-rigid.

12. It is important to distinguish clearly between *absolute shoulds* and other shoulds (e.g., conditional shoulds, recommendatory shoulds, ideal shoulds, empirical shoulds, and shoulds of preference). Target *only* your absolute shoulds for change in REBT, since these are the only shoulds that underpin your disturbed feelings. A typical absolute should is, 'I absolutely should do well at all times at work, no matter what happens.' A typical conditional should is, 'If I want to pass my examination I should work hard.'

13. Whenever you disturb yourself, ask yourself what conditions would have to exist to take your disturbance away. When you have identified these conditions, show yourself that your rigid attitudes towards these conditions are at the core of your disturbance. Examine these rigid attitudes and replace them with flexible attitudes.

14. Rigid and extreme attitudes are often a feature of great works of literature. *Wuthering Heights* is a good example of this. However, just because such attitudes are dramatic and exciting to read about doesn't mean that you need to hold them in your own life. Unless you want to be miserable, that is.

15. If you believe that you absolutely have to have something, you will be disturbed if you do have it because you can always lose it. The healthy alternative is to really want something, but to show yourself that you don't absolutely have to have it.

16. Trying to convince yourself that you don't care about achieving something that you inwardly believe you absolutely must achieve won't work because it is a lie. Rather, convince yourself that you really want to achieve it, but you don't absolutely have to.

17. People often ask me why I write so much. The answer is that I enjoy writing, and I don't demand that I be inspired before writing.

18. There is no reason why people must not do the dirty on you, but there is also no reason why you have to put up with it.

19. The path to mental health is not taken by reducing your high standards but by giving up your rigid attitudes that you must achieve these standards.

If Mozart had consulted me regarding his anxiety about writing his magnum opus, the Requiem Mass, I would not have urged him to give up his plans to write it, nor would I have suggested that he write a few simple sonatas instead. Rather, I would have encouraged him to write his Requiem Mass and to adopt the flexible attitude that while it was important for him to write it, it wasn't an absolute necessity for him to do so.

20. You can ruin even the best of ideas by becoming dogmatic about them.

21. Rigid attitudes are like viruses. You are aware of the effects of viruses but not their existence.

22. Rigid attitudes are like weeds. If you don't regularly uproot them, they will grow back.

23. Remind yourself that when you hold rigid attitudes, you deprive yourself and others of your and their freedom.

24. When you are with others, demanding that you must say something interesting before you speak will lead you to stay silent.

25. You are special to yourself but not special in the universe. So, if you think that the universe has to give you what you want because you are special, you are in for a rude awakening.

26. When you hold rigid attitudes, you are in danger of neglecting your physical and mental health since these attitudes will drive you on at times when it is healthy for you to stop.

27. A major obstacle to emotional growth is dogmatism. But take care, for you can be dogmatic about not being dogmatic.

28. We often think that we are immune from certain negative life events. If one such event happens to us, we say, 'I didn't think that it would ever happen to me.' But we don't have such immunity, nor do we have to have it. If we accept this, we will take due care and attention to avoid such events if we can do so and not disturb ourselves if we cannot.

$$\downarrow$$

29. When we demand that we have to be immune from certain life events, and one such event happens to us, we think we are highly vulnerable to danger. Our perception of increased vulnerability stems from our unmet demand for immunity.

30. When you hold rigid attitudes towards yourself, you abuse yourself. Instead, when you hold flexible attitudes towards yourself, you encourage yourself.

31. Trying to gain the approval of everyone you meet because you hold the attitude that you must have their approval is the best way of losing touch with yourself.

$$\downarrow$$

32. So, give up the need for approval. Wanting approval but realising that you don't need it will help you to be yourself.

33. Procrustes was an innkeeper who held the rigid attitude that his guests had to have a good night's sleep. Holding this attitude and only having one size of bed, he cut off the legs of guests who were too tall for the bed and stretched the guests who were too short for it.

When you are unhealthily angry, you have a similar philosophy to Procrustes. You believe that events must match your conception of how things must be and, consequently, you try angrily to make them fit your Procrustean bed.

The healthy alternative to this is to develop a flexible attitude whereby you acknowledge that it would be nice if things were as you want them to be, but they don't have to fit your size bed.

34. When you respond to others based on rigidity, this is likely to lead to increased rigidity from these others.

35. Be prepared but not rigidly so.

36. Value things without rigidity.

37. Demanding that you mustn't have a problem doesn't get rid of the problem. It doubles your problems.

38. When you hold a rigid attitude, you think you have no options. When you hold a flexible attitude, you can see what your options are.

39. It is useful to distinguish between active caring (where you care and act) and passive caring (where you care but don't act). You don't have to act whenever you care, and you probably don't have the time to do so. Holding the attitude that you must act whenever you care will lead to guilt and often to action paralysis.

40. Holding a rigid attitude leads to black-and-white thinking.

$$\downarrow$$

41. Thus, if you hold the rigid attitude that you have to be in control and you begin to lose control, you will think your loss of control will be total.

$$\downarrow$$

42. Put simply, if you can't convince yourself that you are in full control, you will think you are completely out of control when under the influence of a rigid attitude

43. If you hold a rigid attitude whereby you think that you need to be certain that what you think is a threat is, in fact, benign, then you will think that the threat is very dangerous if you can't convince yourself that it is benign.

44. Put simply again, if you can't convince yourself that you are safe from threat, then you will think you are at the mercy of a great threat when under the influence of a rigid attitude.

45. Travel may broaden the mind, but not if that mind is rigid.

46. When you hold a rigid attitude, you lose sight of the complexity of the context in which you hold this attitude.

47. Input: a rigid attitude
    Output: an extreme attitude and highly distorted negative thinking.

48. No matter how strong your desire is, demanding that you must have this desire met is optional.

49. Living under the influence of a rigid attitude is like driving under the influence of alcohol.

50. Rigid attitudes are like hell. Very easy to get into but very difficult to get out of.

51. It's the imperative that impairs you.

52. It's not the reflection of your face that disturbs you. It's the reflection of your rigid attitude towards your face.

53. It's the got-to that gets you.

54. Holding the rigid attitude that you must not make mistakes is one of the biggest mistakes that you can make.

55. As humans, we make several logical fallacies that harm us psychologically as well as logically.

56. When we make the *is–ought* fallacy, we say that things must be the way they are now going forward into the future. We would still be living in caves if this fallacy were true. Obviously, it is not!

57. When we make the *desire–ought* fallacy. We say that because we want things to be a certain way; therefore, they must be that way. That only works when we control the universe!

58. Put the *F* word into your thinking – flexibility.

59. If your mind is musty, give it a spring clean with flexibility.

60. **Flexible attitudes** ('I want to, but I don't absolutely have to') are healthy for the following reasons:

    a. **They generally yield good results:**
       While a flexible attitude may have one or two poor results (e.g., they may initially be less motivating than demands), by and large, most of the results it yields are good (e.g., it results in healthy rather than unhealthy negative emotions if an adversity is encountered and it is more motivating in the longer run).

    b. **They are true:**
       You can prove that your flexible attitude is true, and it is also true that you do not absolutely have to have what you want.

    c. **They are logical:**
       A flexible attitude (e.g., 'I want to do well, but don't absolutely have to do well') comprises two non-rigid components that are logically connected since both are non-rigid.

61. It is important that you accurately distinguish between rigid and flexible attitudes. In doing so, use the full version of flexible attitudes, which explicitly negates rigidity.

$$\downarrow$$

62. Use the full version of a flexible attitude (e.g., 'I very much want to pass this test, *but I really don't absolutely have to do so'*) rather than the partial version, which does not explicitly negate rigidity (e.g., 'I very much want to pass this test'). If you use the partial version, you are more vulnerable to transforming it into a rigid attitude (e.g., *'I very much want to pass this test...and therefore I absolutely have to do so'*).

63. Construct healthy alternatives to your rigid (and extreme attitudes). In doing so, put these healthy attitudes into your own words.

64. Adopting a flexible attitude to feeling a bit bad will help prevent you from feeling really bad.

65. Mental and emotional fragility are based on rigidity, while mental and emotional strength are based on flexibility.

66. Rigidity and flexibility are culture free.

67. Flexibility enables you to choose to prioritise among equally strongly held values according to the particularities of the situation in which you find yourself.

68. Flexible (and non-extreme) attitudes underpin a psychologically healthy response to adversity.

69. Some people don't listen to their still, small, flexible voice, even when it is screaming loudly in their ear.

70. Almost certainly, there is no absolute certainty.

71. It is healthier to be flexible and wrong than rigid and right.

72. If something happened, it empirically should have happened, for all the conditions were in place for it to happen. For this reason, it makes no sense to demand that what happened absolutely should not have happened. So don't waste time making such demands; rather, learn from what happened so you can prevent it happening again in the future.

73. When a misfortune happens to you it is quite natural for you to exclaim, 'Why me!?' This is often a rhetorical question which *really* means: 'It absolutely should not have happened to me.' Instead, ask, 'Why NOT me?' You will see that there are no good reasons why you should be absolutely immune from such misfortune.

Acknowledging this does not mean that you should not have healthy bad feelings about what has befallen you.

74. Give people the right to be wrong. They will exercise this right whether you give it to them or not.

75. Have you noticed how rigid and extreme popular songs and lyrics can be? You can practise becoming more flexible and non-extreme by rewriting these titles and lyrics. Here's a few to be going on with:

- You're someone even though nobody loves you.
- I can still live (and be happy) if living is without you.
- I don't have to be-e-e-e-e-e perfect.
- I can stand it, when you touch me.
- I'd like your love so bad, but I don't need it.

76. If you have a flexible mind, travel may well broaden it, but you can broaden it by staying at home as well.

77. When you hold flexible attitudes, you give yourself *TLC*. For these attitudes are _t_rue, _l_ogical and _c_onstructive.

78. Seeing is not believing. Seeing that an attitude is flexible does not mean that you believe it.

79. Input: a flexible attitude
    Output: a non-extreme attitude and realistic thinking.

80. It is not unhealthy to have a desire. However, it may be unconstructive to act on the desire if there is no chance of getting that desire met.

81. The world does not have to accommodate to your desires even when these desires are very strong.

82. Hold the negativity without rigidity.

83. The power of strong preferences – being emphatic without being dogmatic.

84. Holding a rigid attitude leads you to think only of what you think you must have. Holding a flexible attitude leads you to recognise that other factors may be important.

85. Rigid (and extreme) attitudes lead you to make global overgeneralisations. Flexible (and non-extreme) attitudes make you mindful of local circumstances.

86. Just because it is an old song, it does not mean that you have to continue to sing it.

87. To get and really appreciate what you want, first give up your need for it.

88. Intrusive thoughts are like sushi on a revolving belt. Just because the food comes around, you don't have to eat it. Just because some thoughts come into your mind, doesn't mean that you have to engage with them.

89. Examine your rigid attitude, then act on your desire if it is appropriate for you to do so.

90. Beware of using words like 'always' and 'never', for they tend to be too limiting. However, do not conclude from this that you should never use the word 'always' or always refrain from using the word 'never'.

91. While and/or is generally better than either/or, this is not universally the case.

3

On Unbearability and Bearability Attitudes

92. If you hold an attitude of unbearability towards adversity, you believe that you cannot bear it.

93. **Unbearability attitudes** ('It is unbearable'; 'I cannot stand it'; 'It's too hard') are unhealthy for the following reasons:

a. **They generally yield poor results**:
   While an unbearability attitude may have some positive results (e.g., it may be motivating), by and large most of the results it yields are poor (e.g., it results in anxiety or anger; thus, its motivating effect is contaminated by these unhealthy negative emotions and with the inefficiency that often goes with them).

b. **They are false**:
   An unbearability attitude means that you will either die, disintegrate or lose the capacity for happiness if what you deem to be intolerable exists. None of these is likely to happen.

c. **They are illogical**:
   An unbearability attitude has two components – a non-extreme component (e.g., 'It's difficult to bear...') and an extreme component ('...therefore it is unbearable'). The latter does not logically follow from the former, since you logically cannot derive something extreme from something that is non-extreme

94. **Bearability attitudes** ('Although it is a struggle to bear, I can bear it. It is worth it to me to bear it, I am worth bearing it for, I am willing to do so and I am committed to doing so') are healthy for the following reasons:

    a. **They generally yield good results**:
        While a bearability attitude may have one or two poor results (e.g., it may initially be less motivating than an unbearability attitude), by and large most of the results it yields are good (e.g., it results in healthy rather than unhealthy negative emotions if adversities are encountered, and is more motivating in the longer run).

    b. **They are true**:
        You can prove that it is struggle to bear not having your preference met; and you can also prove that you can bear doing so, since when your preference is not met (i) you will, in all probability, neither die nor disintegrate, and (ii) you will still retain the capacity for future happiness.

    c. **They are logical**
        An attitude of bearability (e.g., 'Although it is a struggle to bear not doing well, I can bear not doing so. It is worth me bearing it, I am worth bearing it for, I am willing to do so and I am committed to doing so') is made up of six non-extreme components that are logically connected, since all are non-extreme.

95. Developing an attitude of bearability towards adversity involves showing yourself that:

- it is a struggle to bear the adversity
- you can bear it
- it is worth bearing
- you are worth bearing it for
- you are willing to bear it
- you are going to bear it.

96. It is not healthy, therefore, to bear what is not worth bearing.

97. The full version of an attitude of bearability is shown in the following example: 'It would be a struggle to put up with not passing this test, *but it is not unbearable. I can bear the struggle of not passing the test and it is worth it to me to do so. Furthermore, I am worth bearing it for. I am therefore willing to bear the struggle and I am going to do so.*' Use this rather than the partial version which does not explicitly negate the unbearability of the struggle to cope with an adversity (e.g.' It would be a struggle to bear not passing this test'). If you use the partial version, you are more vulnerable to transforming it into an extreme attitude (e.g., 'It would be a struggle to bear not passing this test…and therefore it would be unbearable').

98. Use the 'grim and bear it' method. Show yourself that the adversity you are facing may be grim, but you can bear it.

99. When we make the *struggle–unbearable* fallacy, we say that because we may struggle to bear an adversity, it means that we cannot bear it. However, we can almost always bear the adversity if it is worth it for us to do so and we think we are worth doing it for.

100. You can gain a sense of safety by bearing feeling unsafe.

101. Bearing an adversity does not mean passively putting up with it. You can bear it with taking action or without taking action.

102. Bearing an adversity is a prelude to taking action designed to change it.

103. Being able to bear confusion is the first step towards becoming unconfused.

104. Discomfort is uncomfortable. It's not supposed to be anything else. Bear it only if it is your healthy interests to do so.

105. We often settle for chronic discomfort to avoid acute discomfort. We do so because we think, wrongly, that we cannot bear to experience the acute discomfort. However, if we are prepared to bear the acute discomfort and see that it is in our interests to do so, then we will increase our chances of escaping from chronic discomfort.

4

On Awfulising and Non-Awfulising Attitudes

106.   **Awfulising attitudes** ('It's awful that...'; 'It's terrible that ...'; 'It's the end of the world that...') are unhealthy for the following reasons:

a. **They generally yield poor results**:
   While an awfulising attitude may have some positive results (e.g., it may be motivating), by and large, most of the results it yields are poor (e.g., it results in anxiety or depression; thus, its motivating effect is contaminated by these unhealthy negative emotions and with the inefficiency that often goes with them).

b. **They are false:**
   Awful means nothing could be worse and no good could come from bad. This is untrue since things can virtually always be worse than they are, and good can come from bad. Awful also means that something is so bad that it absolutely must not exist. But no matter how bad it is, it unfortunately does exist.

c. **They are illogical:**
   An awfulising attitude comprises two components – a non-extreme component (e.g., 'It is bad if I do not do well') and an extreme component ('...therefore it is awful'). The latter does not logically follow from the former since you logically cannot derive something extreme from something that is non-extreme.

107.   **Non-awfulising attitudes** ('It is bad, but it isn't awful') are healthy for the following reasons:

a. **They generally yield good results**:
While a non-awfulising attitude may have one or two poor results (e.g., it may initially be less motivating than an awfulising attitude), by and large, most of the results it yields are good (e.g., it results in healthy rather than unhealthy negative emotions if adversities are encountered, and is more motivating in the longer run).

b. **They are true:**
You can prove that it is bad when your preferences are not met; and you can also prove that it isn't awful when this happens, because (i) worse things could always happen, and (ii) good things can come from these bad events.

c. **They are logical**:
A non-awfulising attitude (e.g., 'It is bad when I don't do well, but it isn't awful') comprises two non-extreme components that are logically connected, since both are non-extreme.

108. The full version of a non-awfulising attitude is shown in the following example: 'It is very bad if I do not pass this test, *but it isn't awful if I do not so.*' Use this rather than the partial version, which does not explicitly negate extremity (e.g., 'It is very bad if I do not pass this test'). If you use the partial version, you are more vulnerable to transforming it into an extreme attitude (e.g., 'It is very bad if I do not pass this test…and therefore it is awful if I do not do so.').

109. Awfulising is not cured by experience.

110. A trip to 'horror' is a return journey. When you get there, you can come back.

111. Adversities are not the end of the world. They are, unfortunately, part of the world.

112. People often think that the healthy alternative to awfulising is indifference. It is not. The healthy alternative to awfulising is non-awfulising: acknowledging that a negative event is bad but not the end of the world. Indifference means regarding something as neither bad nor good. Thus, to be indifferent about something negative is not healthy.

113. When we make the *bad–awful* fallacy, we say that because it is bad for something to occur, it means that it is awful if it does – meaning that it could not be worse. However, as Smokey Robinson's mother used to tell him, 'Son, from the day you are born till you ride in the hearse, there's nothing so bad that it couldn't be worse.'

114. There is no evil from which some good doesn't come.

115. You can take the horror out of badness, not the badness out of badness.

5

On Devaluation and Acceptance Attitudes

116. **Devaluation attitudes** ('I am bad'; 'You are bad'; 'Life is bad') are unhealthy for the following reasons:

a. **They generally yield poor results:**
   While an extreme devaluation attitude may have some positive results (e.g., they may be motivating), by and large, most of the results it yields are poor (e.g., they result in depression, shame, guilt, hurt, and the unhealthy forms of anger, jealousy and envy; thus its motivating effect is contaminated by these unhealthy negative emotions and with the inefficiency that often goes with them).

b. **They are false:**
   Devaluation attitudes imply that you can legitimately assign a single global rating to a complex being or to the world. You cannot truthfully do this, since you, for example, are too complex to merit such a rating and you are constantly changing.

c. **They are illogical:**
   A devaluation attitude has two components – a rating of a part (e.g., 'I acted badly') and a rating of the whole (e.g., I am bad.') A part cannot define the whole, and thus devaluation attitudes are illogical since they make the part–whole error.

117. When we make the *part–whole* fallacy, we say that we can legitimately rate ourselves, for example, based on our rating of an aspect of ourselves or of an experience that happened to us. However, we cannot legitimately do this as we are far too complex to merit such a global self-rating.

118. If you overvalue money, you think that people's worth is dependent on their financial worth.

119. When you think you are worthless, you act as if you are worthless. Others may then treat you as though you are worthless, which reinforces your idea that you are worthless.

120. When you condemn yourself for something, ask yourself whether or not you would condemn your best friend for the very same thing. If not, why not treat yourself as your own best friend?

121. Do you believe that you are unlovable? The problem lies in your relationship with yourself, not in others' opinion of you. Once you have begun to accept yourself as a fallible human being with a mixture of good, bad and neutral points, you will begin to acknowledge that others can find you lovable.

122. Are you afraid of making a fool of yourself? Well, I've got good news for you. You can't do it. Certainly, you can do something foolish, but that just proves that you are a fallible human being who can act foolishly.

   If you were a fool, all you could do in life would be to act foolishly. It would only take one non-foolish act to prove that you weren't a fool. Reading this book is just such an act!

   Since you're not a fool, you can't make a fool of yourself.

123. Nobody can make you feel inadequate without your agreement that you are inadequate.

124. When you compare yourself to another, make sure that the comparison is focused on something specific and tangible, like a skill, for example. Doing so will enable you to learn from the comparison if you discover that the other person is better at the skill than you are.

125. By contrast, when you compare yourself to another, don't focus on your 'self' and the 'self' of the other. Otherwise, you might wrongly conclude that the other person is better than you, not only at the skill but as a person.

126. If someone rejects you, they may be saying more about their desires than about you. However, they may be giving you valuable feedback about an aspect of you that may turn off other people, too. If you let go of the attitude that being rejected means that you are a rotten person, you will be able to think objectively about which of these two possibilities best explains the rejection.

127. Are you scared of rejection? If you are, it may come as a surprise to you to learn that you are probably more scared of self-rejection than you are of being rejected by others. For if you accepted yourself in the face of rejection by others, would you still be scared of rejection?

128. Self-rejection is often the root of the fear of rejection by others.

129. Unconditional acceptance of self is the healthy response to rejection from others.

130. **Unconditional acceptance attitudes** ('I am fallible and in flux'; 'You are fallible and in flux'; 'Life is a complex mixture of good, bad, and neutral events') are healthy for the following reasons:

a. **They generally yield good results:**
   While an unconditional acceptance attitude may have one or two poor results (e.g., it may initially be less motivating than conditional acceptance attitudes), by and large most of the results it yields are good (e.g., it results in healthy rather than unhealthy negative emotions if adversities are encountered, and is more motivating in the longer run).

b. **They are true:**
   With an attitude of unconditional acceptance, you do not assign a single global rating to a complex being or to the world both of which are in a state of flux.

c. **They are logical**:
   An attitude of unconditional acceptance has two components:

   (i) a rating of a part (e.g., 'I acted badly') or what has happened to you (e.g., 'Being rejected is bad'), and (ii) an acknowledgement that you or your life defies a single global rating (e.g., 'I am a fallible human being who can act well or badly.') The complexity of yourself or your life, along with the changeability characteristic of both, means that a part of yourself or your experience can be incorporated into the whole, but does not define the whole. Thus, unconditional acceptance attitudes are logical since they do not make the part–whole error.

131. When you think people are judging you negatively it may be because you judge yourself negatively.

132. When people do judge you negatively, don't make their judgements of you your judgement of you.

133. Don't try to improve yourself because you just can't do it. You can improve specific things about yourself, but your whole self is far too complex to be improved.

134. If you are reading this in a room, take a look around you and try to give the room one global rating, that completely accounts for it in all its complexity. You can't do it, can you? Why not? Because the room is too complex to be given a single rating. So, if you can't rate a room, how can you rate a human being who is far more complex than a room?

The answer is that you can't – at least legitimately.

135. This is one reason why the concept of self-esteem is problematic. For it involves you giving your 'self' a single rating (or estimation) that completely accounts for it, which, of course, cannot be legitimately done.

136. When asked what I do for a living, I often unthinkingly say that I am a psychologist. The 'I am' bit is the problem here, for it points to my identity, whereas 'psychologist' is only one of many roles that I perform in life. So, to emphasise my complexity as a human being and when I have my wits about me when asked what I do for a living, I will reply: I work as a psychologist.

137. Making anything about you a statement of your identity is a vulnerability factor for psychological disturbance.

138. So, what is the healthy alternative to self-esteem? The answer is unconditional self-acceptance. When you accept yourself without conditions, you acknowledge that you are a complex, unique, fallible human being who cannot be given a single rating, but whose specific aspects can be rated.

139. But what if you want to continue esteeming yourself? How can you do this without getting into emotional trouble? The only way to do this is to make your self-esteem unconditional. Show yourself that you are worthwhile, for example, because you are alive, fallible and unique – conditions which will not change in your lifetime. Of course, this does entail making a leap of faith, for you could equally argue that you are worthless because you are alive, fallible and unique. But if you are prepared to make this

leap and apply unconditional self-esteem consistently, it will help you.

140. The real problem with self-esteem is when it is used conditionally, e.g., I am worthwhile if... (I am successful, I am loved, I do well at work, etc.). If you place conditions on your self-esteem, you will be emotionally disturbed if these conditions aren't met, and you will be vulnerable to emotional disturbance when the conditions are met because they can always be unmet again.

141. Do not attach a label to yourself since it is too limiting and may prevent you from changing. I used to think of myself as a stammerer, and this label prevented me from speaking more fluently. It was also untrue, for even when my stammer was at its worst, I spoke fluently more often than I stammered.

142. You are no better than anyone else. But you are no worse, either.

143. Make 'fallible' the only adjective you use to describe yourself and others.

144. You are not a good person, but parts of you are good.

145. You are not a bad person, but parts of you are bad.

146. You are not an average person, but parts of you are average.

147. So, who are you? You are a unique mixture of the good, the bad and the average.

148. 'Who am I?' is an unanswerable question. Questions such as 'What do I value?' and 'What are my qualities?' are answerable. So, stop asking yourself who you are.

149. You are unique. There will never be another you. Even if we cloned you, you and your clone would be different because you would have different experiences.

150. You are unique. Just like everybody else.

151. Do you think you are stupid? If you really were a stupid person, stupidity would be your essence. This would mean that the only things you could do in life would be stupid things. This is hardly likely. You are not a stupid person; you are a fallible human being who is capable of acting stupidly and non-stupidly.

152. You are not a boring person. But you do have the capacity to bore some people and interest others.

153. If you really were unlovable, this would mean that nobody would be able to love you. This is hardly likely. The truth is that you are both lovable and unlovable, meaning that some people will be able to love you and others won't. Do you know anyone who is either lovable or unlovable?

154. There are no winners and losers in life. There are only people who win and lose at certain things. So don't label yourself or other people based on wins and losses.

155. Would you build a house without strong foundations? Of course not. Then why build a life without recognising and honouring your own strengths?

156. Do you ever think that you are not good enough? Who aren't you good enough for? If you consider carefully you will realise that that person is you.

157. If you truly accept yourself unconditionally, warts and all, you will surely think that you are good enough.

158. Showing yourself compassion means treating yourself as you would a best friend.

159. Appreciate yourself, particularly when others don't appreciate you.

160. Be the best you can be, not the best that it is possible to be. Unless you are Usain Bolt.

161. It's healthy to feel bad about doing something bad because the badness is in the doing it, not in the you for doing it. There's a difference between 'It's bad' and 'I'm bad.'

162. Using another person to bolster your self-esteem is like building a house without foundations.

163. Unhealthy self-control = Attempts to eliminate experience.
Healthy self-control = Accepting and allowing experience.

164. Recognise that when you accept yourself unconditionally for acting badly, you are not letting yourself off the hook or excusing your actions. Rather, you are taking full responsibility for your behaviour but without devaluing yourself for doing what you did.

165. Unconditional acceptance also does not encourage complacency, as some people think. When you are complacent, you think that you and things are OK and that there is no need to change anything. While unconditional acceptance is based upon an acknowledgement of reality about yourself and about what is going on, it does not preclude you from trying to change negative aspects of yourself or of life if these can be changed.

166. Some people are reluctant to 'accept' reality because they believe that acceptance means resignation. It does not. Acceptance really means:

- Acknowledging that an event (normally a negative event) has occurred.

- Evaluating the event as bad.
- Recognising that all the conditions were in place that led to the event occurring.
- Noting that you cannot change these past conditions, but that you may be able to change the conditions that currently exist and, if you can, striving determinedly to do so.

Resignation means that you do nothing to try and change what currently exists.

167. Realise that when you accept someone unconditionally for acting badly, you are not condoning that person's behaviour. You are disliking or hating the sin but accepting unconditionally the person who committed it as a fallible human being who committed a sin.

6

On Psychological Disturbance

168. If you are adamant that very adverse events have caused your emotional problems, it is important that you distinguish between the origin and maintenance of emotional problems. Even if you are correct in stating that the adversities in question originally caused your emotional problems, you are still actively keeping this disturbance alive in the present by the rigid and extreme attitudes that you hold now towards events that happened then. Please note that you can do something now to change these presently held rigid and extreme attitudes.

169. The problem is not your unhealthy thinking. The problem is your unchecked unhealthy thinking.

170. Disturbing yourself about unfairness is doubly unfair. First, you are being treated unfairly by others. Second, you treat yourself unfairly by disturbing yourself about the first unfairness.

171. The inferences we make about ourselves, others and the world are heavily influenced by our attitudes towards ourselves, other people and the world.

172. When you disturb yourself about an adversity, you add self-inflicted insult to external injury.

173. When you insist on banning all doubt, you get the certainty of self-disturbance.

174. When you have an emotional problem about an emotional problem, this is known in REBT as a meta-emotional problem. Meta-emotional problems are like interfering radio stations, making it difficult for you to focus on the station you need to listen to and focus on.

175. People react more to what they have lost than to what they possess.

176. OCD – the failed attempt to gain some kind of purity but continuing rigidly to try to get it.

177. OCD – perpetuation of the problem by desperate attempts at elimination.

178. You may not always be able to prevent yourself from beginning to disturb yourself, but you can stop yourself from continuing to disturb yourself.

179. Holding flexible attitudes towards life's adversities leads to you experiencing negative but healthy emotions towards these adversities. These healthy emotions may well be very powerful. However, they are still healthy.

180. When we face an adversity, it is healthy to feel bad about it. In REBT, such emotions are known as healthy negative emotions. Such emotions encourage you to face and deal effectively with adversity, change it if it can be changed and adjust constructively to it if it can't be changed.

181. Examples of healthy negative emotions are: non-anxious concern, non-depressed sadness, shame-free disappointment, guilt-free remorse, hurt-free sorrow and the healthy forms of anger, regret, jealousy and envy.

182. However, we may feel unhealthily bad about an adversity. In REBT, such emotions are known as unhealthy negative emotions. Such emotions discourage you from facing adversity or lead you to deal ineffectively with it.

183. When this happens, we hold a set of rigid and extreme attitudes towards the adversity.

184. Examples of unhealthy negative emotions are: anxiety, depression, shame, guilt, hurt and the unhealthy forms of anger, regret, jealousy and envy.

185. Thus, you need to help yourself to feel healthily bad about an adversity rather than to feel good or neutral about it.

186. People often want to feel less of an unhealthy negative emotion (e.g., less anxiety). This occurs when they don't understand that a healthy negative emotion option is available (e.g., non-anxious concern).

187. People often disturb themselves about their unhealthy negative emotions. They do so because they hold rigid and extreme attitudes towards these emotions. Here, the goal is first to help such people to undisturb themselves about having the unhealthy negative emotions before helping them to address the latter.

188. In understanding your disturbed emotions, you may find it useful to understand the concept of the 'personal domain'. This is a psychological space in which matters you deem important are located. The more central something is located within your personal domain, the more likely it is that you will disturb yourself if it is threatened, for example; but only when you hold

a rigid and extreme attitude towards the threat.

189. Your personal domain is unique to you. Thus, no two people have the same personal domain.

190. You may mistake your feelings with your inferences. Thus, you may say that you 'feel rejected', 'feel insulted' or 'feel criticised'. In reality, you have been rejected, insulted or criticised open brackets or think or think that you have been, and you have feelings about these adversities.

In the next nine parts, I will discuss the main nine troublesome emotions for which people seek help, their healthy alternatives and the adversities that these different emotions are associated with.

7

On Anxiety

191. If you want to overcome anxiety, you first need to understand what leads to this emotion. Anxiety stems in part from the inference that:

- You are facing a *threat* to some important aspect of your personal domain

But anxiety really comes from the rigid and extreme attitudes that you hold towards this inference. Namely:

- 'This threat must not exist and if it materialises, it would be awful, unbearable and prove that I am unworthy.'

192. There are basically two types of anxiety: discomfort anxiety (DA) and ego anxiety (EA). Anxiety arises when you hold rigid and extreme attitudes towards threats to your sense of comfort (DA) or to your self-esteem (EA).

193. Discomfort anxiety stems from the rigid and extreme attitude that conditions in your life must not be uncomfortable and it is terrible if they are.

194. Ego anxiety stems from the rigid and extreme attitude that you must do well and be approved and that you are worthless if you do poorly or are disapproved.

195. When you are anxious you tend to act in the following ways. You will avoid the threat, withdraw from it, or engage in a range of safety-seeking behaviours.

196. When you are anxious you tend to think in the following ways. You will exaggerate the nature of the threat and its consequences and you will tend to underestimate your ability to deal with the threat.

197. You may be reluctant to give up your feelings of anxiety for several reasons. You may be so reluctant because you have taught yourself to motivate yourself through these feelings. Anxiety will motivate you, but in a mindless, 'headless-chicken' kind of way, based as it is on rigid and extreme attitudes. On the other hand, concern (the healthy alternative to anxiety) will motivate you, but in a healthy, clear-minded, determined way, based on flexible and non-extreme attitudes. You may not be used to motivating yourself through concern, but you can learn to do so. In the long term, using concern rather than anxiety as a prime motivator will be worth it.

198. Non-anxious concern is the healthy alternative to anxiety. In concern, you make the same inference as in anxiety, namely:

- You are facing a *threat* to some important aspect of your personal domain.

But when you feel concern, you hold a different set of attitudes than when you feel anxious. These attitudes are flexible and non-extreme in nature. Namely:

- 'I don't want this threat to exist, but that does not mean that it must not do so. If it materialises, it would be bad but not awful, I would bear it and I can accept myself unconditionally as a fallible human being.

199. When you are healthily concerned you tend to act in the following ways. You will face the threat, look at it and not withdraw from it. You will refrain from engaging in a range of safety-seeking behaviours.

200. When you are healthily concerned tend to think in the following ways. You will think realistically and in a balanced way about the nature of the threat and its consequences and you will tend to have a realistic view of your ability to deal with the threat.

201. The healthy alternative to anxiety is concern, not calmness. If you are faced with a threat, you want to mobilise yourself to deal with it. Concern will help you to do this; calmness won't.

202. Consequently, don't reduce your anxiety. Transform it into non-anxious concern in the face of threat by developing a set of flexible and non-extreme attitudes.

203. When you feel anxious, you will experience a strong tendency to withdraw from the threat or to avoid situations where it may occur. However, you don't have to act on this tendency. Rather, you can use it to deal with your anxiety-creating attitude.

204. Withdrawal and avoidance lead to the perpetuation of anxiety. Why? Because every time you withdraw from or avoid a threatening situation, you rehearse and thereby strengthen the rigid and extreme attitudes that underpin your anxiety, and you deprive yourself of the experience of dealing with the threat should it come to pass.

205. If you can't withdraw from or avoid the threat, you may find yourself trying to distract yourself from it. People think that it is good to distract yourself from threat because it lowers your anxiety. This may happen, but distraction is only helpful in the very short term. Its use often prevents you (1) from facing the threat fair and square and dealing with it and (2) from identifying, examining and changing the rigid and extreme attitudes that largely determine your anxiety.

206. Are you anxious? Do you demand guarantees in life? The only guarantee that I will give you is this: I guarantee that you will remain anxious as long as you demand a guarantee. The healthy alternative is to acknowledge that while you might want a guarantee, you don't need one. Once you hold this flexible attitude, you will see much more clearly that such guarantees do not exist.

207. Do you think that you need a guarantee that everything will turn out for the best? Yes? OK, then here it is: I guarantee that everything will turn out for the best. Happy now? No? Then perhaps the problem is in your attitude that you need a guarantee.

208. The next time someone tells you not to worry, ask them for precise instructions of how you can do this.

209. Feelings of anxiety lead to an exaggeration of threat, which may well, in turn, result in increased anxiety.

210. If you try desperately to control your anxiety, you will only succeed in increasing your anxiety. The problem here is your desperation. Thus, if you want to control your anxiety, do so without desperation.

211. Anxiety can be a very painful feeling, but it is not an 'end of the world' experience. If you regard it as such you will transform your anxiety into panic. So, if you don't want to panic, take the horror out of anxiety.

212. It is good to be in control, but if you demand that you must be in control you will be anxious when you begin to lose control. Also, demanding that you must be in control will lead you to overestimate the degree to which you will lose control. Thus, people who hold rigid attitudes towards self-control think that they are either in control or totally out of control. They envisage themselves falling apart or ending up a gibbering wreck in a psychiatric hospital.

However, if you hold a flexible attitude towards self-control whereby you want to be in control, but this is not a necessity, then you will see that control lies on a continuum and is not an either/or experience. Thus, if you begin to lose control, you will be concerned about this but not frightened by it. This attitude will help you to regain control.

213. People often try to relax when they are anxious. This is not necessarily a bad idea, but use relaxation techniques after you have identified, examined and changed your anxiety-creating attitudes. If you try to relax without first changing these attitudes, you may help yourself on this one occasion, but you will render yourself vulnerable to anxiety in the future because your anxiety-creating attitudes remain intact.

214. If there is anything certain in the universe it is that there is no certainty. Yet innumerable people demand certainty. A common example of this is the demand to know instantly that an unexplained symptom is benign. People who make such a demand come to think that a state of uncertainty means something is wrong with them. Only when they give up this demand can they see that uncertainty is not synonymous with illness. In fact, it is very common to have an unexplained symptom that is benign. This does not mean that we should ignore unexplained symptoms. It is healthy to be concerned and vigilant, and being so will help us wait and see what happens and take steps if the symptom does not clear up. However, we can't do this if we demand instant certainty that there is nothing wrong with us. This attitude will lead us to constantly seek reassurance which we do not believe. This is because when we demand certainty, we are not reassurable.

215. When you are anxious you not only overestimate the degree of threat you are facing, you also underestimate your ability to cope with the threat. So, after you have identified, examined and changed the attitudes that are at the core of your anxiety, develop a list of your coping resources and regularly put these resources into practice until you have increased your confidence in your ability to cope.

216. Courage is taking constructive action even though you feel afraid.

217. If you consider that you can stop something from happening by worrying about it, you are deluding yourself and seducing yourself into a lifetime of worry.

218. Security resides in an attitude that you take towards something. It does not reside in possessing the thing itself. Even if you possess something you think makes you secure, you could always lose it. But if you want it but don't need it, then you are secure whether you have it or not.

219. Nobody is afraid of flying. You may be afraid that the plane may crash or that you may lose control or be uncertain about what will happen to you. But nobody has ever said: 'Oh my God, the plane that I am going on might fly.'

220. Worry is an attempt to work out now what you can't work out now. But this realisation does not stop you from trying to work it out.

221. If you want to stop worrying, strive to take the horror out of everything, but not the badness. But realise that you cannot do this perfectly once and for all. It is a process, not an outcome.

222. When you worry, you frequently ask yourself 'what if...' questions. When you do so, assume that the 'what if?' will happen and do two things: (1) take the horror out of it, and (2) prove to yourself that you can deal with it even though it will probably be difficult.

223. People who worry are like novel readers who close the book at the scary bits. To stop worrying go through the scary bits and get to the novel's end.

224. Did you hear about what happened to the man who was so scared of life that he took to his bed, believing that he was safe there? He was killed by a broken spring in his mattress!

225. There is no place in the world that is absolutely safe. Believing that you need to be absolutely safe is what keeps you anxious.

226. When you feel anxious, you have basically two options: to go forward and confront what you are scared of or go backwards and avoid it. Which of these two options is more comfortable, and which is likely to lead you to overcome your anxiety? The answers to these two questions are different.

227. So, if you want to overcome anxiety, accept that the best way to do so is to go forward and confront threat. This will be the more uncomfortable of the two options, but only in the short term.

228. Worrying about a loved one is not a sign of love. It is a sign of disturbance.

229. Our relationship with anxiety is often based on our need to eliminate it. However, since anxiety thrives on attempts to get rid of it, this will only result in our becoming more anxious, not less. For now, we fear our feelings of anxiety as well as whatever we were anxious about in the first place.

230. In public speaking, it is important to determine whether you are primarily anxious about your judgement of your performance or about others' judgement of your performance.

231. Anxiety is painful and an inconvenience. It is there to alert you to the fact that you are inferring the presence of a threat. Should the threat exist, it's not there to stop you from doing anything productive about dealing with it, although non-anxious concern will help you deal better with the threat than anxiety.

232. If anxiety is fire, your attitude to it is either rigid and extreme or flexible and non-extreme. The former attitude is like oil, which increases anxiety, while the latter attitude is like water, which helps you to put out the fire.

233. When you're anxious, reassurance will not help you since you are probably not reassurable.

234. An anxiety-related intrusive thought is like a narcissist; deprived of attention, it will go away.

235. Anxiety is not an impediment to productive action. However, non-anxious concern will make it easier for you to act productively.

236. Anxiety results from the clash between reality and your demand that reality must not exist.

237. More psychological problems are brought about by desperate attempts to conceal or eliminate anxiety than by the anxiety itself.

8

On Depression

238. If you want to overcome depression, you first need to understand what leads to this emotion. Depression stems in part from the inference that:

- I have suffered a *loss* or *failure* within my personal domain.
- An *undeserved plight* that has happened to me or others.

But depression really comes from the rigid and extreme attitudes that you hold towards these inferences. Namely:

- I must not have suffered a loss or failure within my personal domain.
- An undeserved plight must not have happened to me or others.
- It is terrible if such adversities happen and they prove that (a) I am unworthy or a poor person to be pitied or (b) that others are poor people to be pitied.

239. Three zones of your personal domain are important in understanding depression: the autonomous zone, the sociotropic zone and the plight zone.

240. If you experience autonomous depression, you have lost autonomy in some important aspect of your life or have failed to achieve important goals and, as shown above, you hold a set of rigid and extreme attitudes towards this loss/failure.

241. If you experience sociotropic depression, you have lost connection with an important person or group of people and again, as shown above you hold a set of rigid and extreme attitudes towards this loss.

242. If you experience plight-based depression, you or others have experienced a plight which you consider undeserved and, again, you hold a set of rigid and extreme attitudes towards this undeserved plight.

243. When you feel depression. you will tend to act in the following ways.

- You become overly dependent on and seek to cling to others (particularly in sociotropic depression).
- You bemoan your fate or that of others to anyone who will listen (particularly in pity-based depression).
- You create an environment consistent with your depressed feelings.
- You attempt to terminate feelings of depression in self-destructive ways.
- You either push away attempts to comfort you (in autonomous depression) or use such comfort to reinforce your dependency (in sociotropic depression) or your self- or other-pity (in pity-based depression).

244. When you feel depressed, you will tend to think in the following ways:

- You see only negative aspects of the loss, failure or undeserved plight.
- You think of other losses, failures and undeserved plights that you (and in the case of the latter, others) have experienced.
- You think you are unable to help yourself (helplessness).
- You only see pain and blackness in the future (hopelessness).
- You see yourself being totally dependent on others (in autonomous depression).
- You see yourself as being disconnected from others (in sociotropic depression).
- You see the world as full of undeservedness and unfairness (in plight-based depression).
- You tend to ruminate concerning the source of your depression and its consequences.

245. Depression-free sadness is the healthy alternative to depression. In depression-free sadness, you make the same inference as in shame, namely:

- I have suffered a *loss* or *failure* within my personal domain.
- An *undeserved plight* that has happened to me or others.

But when you feel depression-free sadness, you hold a different set of attitudes than when you feel depression. These attitudes are flexible and non-extreme in nature, namely:

- I really did not want to suffer a loss or failure within my personal domain, but sadly, that does not mean that these adversities must not happen to me.

- It would be much better if an undeserved plight does not happen to me or others but that does not mean that they must not happen.
- It is bad, but not terrible if such adversities happen. They do not prove that (a) I am unworthy or a poor person to be pitied or (b) that others are poor people to be pitied. It proves that we are all fallible humans who are not immune from such adversities or undeserved plight and neither do we have to be immune from them.

246. When you feel sadness, you will tend to act in the following ways:

- You seek out reinforcements after a period of mourning (particularly when your inferential theme is loss).
- You create an environment inconsistent with depressed feelings.
- You express your feelings about the loss, failure or undeserved plight and talk in a non-complaining way about these feelings to significant others.
- You allow yourself to be comforted in a way that helps you to express your feelings of sadness and mourn your loss.

247. When you feel sadness, you will tend to think in the following realistic and balanced ways:

- You are able to recognise both negative and positive aspects of the loss or failure.
- You think you are able to help yourself.
- You look to the future with hope.

248. Consequently, don't reduce your depression. Transform it into non-depressed sadness in the face of loss/failure/undeserved plight by developing a set of flexible and non-extreme attitudes.

249. People don't get depressed by facts. Rather, they depress themselves by the rigid and extreme attitudes they hold towards these facts.

250. You may be reluctant to give up your feelings of depression for several reasons. You may be so reluctant because you think that it is an appropriate response to a significant loss and that sadness minimises the significance of your loss. However, depression is a disturbed response to a loss because it is based on rigid and extreme attitudes and involves withdrawal from life and despair about the future. Your rejecting sadness as an appropriate response to your loss may be based on the idea that it is a mild or moderate emotion. However, it can be an intense emotion that allows you to digest your loss without withdrawing from life or despairing about the future.

251. Depression loves inactivity. Before you deal with your depression-related attitudes be as active as you can be.

252. In the early 1980s, I applied for 54 jobs and got none of them. People said, 'How depressing for you', but they were wrong. For I experienced 54 job rejections and zero self-rejections.

253. Don't forget. When you lose something important to you, it's healthy to feel sad. Don't try to feel nothing. The only way to do this is to persuade yourself that you don't care what you do care about.

254. Trying to solve a problem when you are depressed is like walking up a steep hill with both feet tied together.

255. You keep your feelings of self-pity alive by telling people how terrible it is that you have been treated so badly and by them agreeing with you. So, if you want to tell others about your plight, do *not* agree with them that (a) you absolutely should not have been treated so badly and (b) it is terrible that this happened.

256. When others treat you badly and you do not deserve such treatment, recognise that their behaviour is governed by what is in their heads rather than by what you deserve.

257. If there is a planet where justice and fairness exist as a matter of course, it is not called Earth.

258. Dealing healthily with unfairness and injustice is one of the most difficult things to cope with. So don't make it any harder by demanding that, because you don't deserve it, unfairness or injustice absolutely must not happen to you. Rather, acknowledge that you are not immune from such unfairness or injustice, no matter how undeserving you are and that you do not have to have such immunity. This will help you to focus on righting the wrong.

259. The first step to overcoming self-pity is to stop feeling ashamed of feeling sorry for yourself.

260. The next step to overcoming self-pity involves swallowing a bitter pill. It means fully accepting that while you do not deserve to be treated badly, there is no earthly reason why you must be exempt from such bad treatment.

261. Imagine that you are a refugee in a refugee camp. Would you want to be helped by an aid worker who is affected by, but not terribly depressed about, your plight, or by one who is very depressed about what is happening to you?

You would probably want to be helped by the former rather than the latter. Why? Because the aid worker who is terribly depressed won't be able to help you efficiently. This explains why other-pity is unproductive to both the person pitying and the person being pitied.

262. The need to impress leads to the tendency to depress.

263. Misery loves company, but company does not love misery.

9

On Shame

264. If you want to overcome shame, you first need to understand what leads to this emotion. Shame stems in part from the inference that:

- *I have fallen very short of my ideal* within my personal domain before a real or imagined audience.
- *Others will look down on me or shun me if I fall short of my ideal.*

But shame really comes from the rigid and extreme attitudes that you hold towards these inferences. Namely:

- I must not fall very short of my ideal before an actual or imagined audience.
- I am defective, diminished or disgraceful as a person if I fall very short of my ideal and/or if others look down on me or shun me.

265. When you feel shame, you will tend to act in the following ways.

- You remove yourself from the 'gaze' of others.
- You isolate yourself from others.
- You save face by attacking other(s) who have 'shamed' you.
- You defend your threatened self-esteem in self-defeating ways.
- You ignore attempts by others to restore social equilibrium.

266. When you feel shame, you will tend to think in the following ways:

- You overestimate the negativity of the information revealed.
- You overestimate the likelihood that the judging group will notice or be interested in the information.
- You overestimate the degree of disapproval you (or your reference group) will receive.
- You overestimate how long any disapproval will last.

267. Shame-free disappointment is the healthy alternative to shame. In shame, you make the same inference as in shame, namely:

- *I have fallen very short of my ideal* within my personal domain before a real or imagined audience.
- *Others will look down on me or shun me if I fall short of my ideal.*

But when you feel shame-free disappointment, you hold a different set of attitudes than when you feel shame. These attitudes are flexible and non-extreme in nature. Namely:

- I really don't want to feel short of my ideal within my personal domain, but this does not mean that this must not happen.
- If I fall very short of my ideal and/or if others look down on me or shun me, I am not defective, diminished or disgraceful. I am an ordinary fallible being no matter if I reach my standards or not or whether or not others look down on me or shun me.

268. When you feel disappointment, you will tend to act in the following ways:

- You continue to participate actively in social interaction.
- You respond positively to attempts of others to restore social equilibrium.

↓

269. When you feel disappointment, you will tend to think in the following realistic and balanced ways:

- You see the information revealed in a compassionate self-accepting context.
- You are realistic about the likelihood that the judging group will notice or be interested in the information revealed.
- You are realistic about the degree of disapproval self (or reference group) will receive.
- You are realistic about how long any disapproval will last.

270. You may be reluctant to give up your feelings of shame for several reasons. You may be so reluctant because you think that the threat of feeling shame will motivate you to achieve your ideal. Actually, it won't. The threat of shame will lead you to feel anxious about possibly experiencing shame and, rather than help you to concentrate upon what you are doing, will interfere with your performance – which in turn almost guarantees that you will fall short of your ideal. Disappointment (the healthy alternative to shame) is as healthily motivating as concern (see point 195) and, while it won't guarantee that you will achieve your ideal, it will help you to come as close as you can.

271. One of the main differences between shame and guilt lies in your experience of yourself in terms of size and power. In guilt, you often experience yourself as a big, powerful, bad person who has harmed or hurt others. In shame, you often experience yourself as a small, insignificant worm who hopes to disappear entirely from public view.

272. Another major difference between shame and guilt concerns what you fear. In shame, you fear exclusion from the social group when, whereas in guilt, you fear that your social group will be other sinners in hell.

273. Shame represents the failed attempt to exclude a part of yourself that you devalue yourself for.

274. Shame is a major reason why people don't deal with their emotional problems. Feeling ashamed about having an emotional means that you are more likely to push the issue away than to deal with it.

275. Some people feel ashamed about feeling ashamed. You can even feel ashamed about your shame about your shame! As human beings, we are often very creative in the way that we deepen our disturbances.

276. Accepting yourself unconditionally as a complex, unratable, unique human being with strengths, weaknesses, and neutral aspects is thus the best antidote to shame.

277. Do you think thoughts that you feel ashamed about? If so, don't try to stop them. Trying not to think about something will only increase these thoughts. Instead, give up your rigid attitude that you must not have these thoughts and then let them go of their own accord.

278. Do you fear losing self-control? If so, you are likely ashamed of doing so. Shame is based on the rigid attitude that you must be in control of yourself at all times and if not, you are a weak person.
    The healthy alternative is to develop the flexible attitude that, while perfect personal control may be desirable, it is neither necessary nor possible. When you hold this attitude and you begin to lose control, you will view this as evidence that you are

an ordinary human being and not a weak person.

This anti-shame attitude will lead you to feel unanxiously concerned about the prospect of losing self-control, but not panicked about doing so.

279. Pride comes before a shame. They are both based on rigid and extreme self-evaluative attitudes. You evaluate yourself positively when you feel proud about achieving your ideal, but when you don't, you feel shame because you evaluate yourself negatively.

$$\downarrow$$

280. Consequently, it is important to work towards evaluating behaviour while accepting yourself unconditionally as an antidote to both pride and shame.

281. Shame and guilt are disorders of identity. In shame, you consider yourself to be defective, disgusting or diminished. In guilt, you consider yourself to be bad.

10

On Guilt

282. If you want to overcome guilt you first need to understand what leads to this emotion. Guilt stems in part from the inference that:

- I have *done the wrong thing* (sin of commission).
- I have *failed to do the right thing* (sin of omission).
- I have *harmed someone or hurt their feelings.*

But guilt really comes from the rigid and extreme attitudes that you hold towards these inferences. Namely:

- I must not do the wrong thing. I am a bad person if I do what I absolutely should not have done.
- I must do the right thing. I am a bad person if I don't do what I absolutely should have done.
- I must not harm another or hurt their feelings. I am a bad person if I harm someone or hurt their feelings.

283. When you feel guilt, you will tend to act in the following ways. You will beg the person you have wronged for forgiveness and engage in self-punishing behaviour.

284. When you feel guilt, you will tend to think in the following ways. You will assume far more responsibility than is warranted. You will give others far less responsibility than is warranted, and you will not take into account mitigating factors.

↓

285. Guilt-free remorse is the healthy alternative to guilt. In guilt-free remorse you make the same inferences as in guilt, namely:

- I have *done the wrong thing* (sin of commission).
- I have *failed to do the right thing* (sin of omission).
- I have *harmed someone or hurt their feelings*.

But when you feel remorse, you hold a different set of attitudes than when you feel guilt. These attitudes are flexible and non-extreme in nature. Namely:

- I wish I hadn't done the wrong thing, but there's no reason why I absolutely should not have done it. I am a fallible human being who did the wrong thing. I am not a bad person.
- I wish I had done the right thing, but there's no reason why I absolutely should have done it. I am a fallible human being who failed to do the right thing. I am not a bad person.
- I wish I had not harmed the other person or hurt their feelings, but there's no reason why I absolutely should not have done so. I am a fallible human being for doing so. I am not a bad person.

↓

286. When you feel guilt-free remorse, you will tend to act in the following ways:

- You will ask the other person for forgiveness but will not beg them.
- You may penalise yourself but will not punish yourself.

↓

287. When you feel guilt-free remorse, you will tend to think in the following realistic and balanced ways:

- You will assign yourself and others the appropriate amount of responsibility.
- You will take into account mitigating factors.

288. Guilt = responsibility + self-blame
Guilt-free remorse = responsibility + unconditional self-acceptance

289. You may be reluctant to give up your feelings of guilt for a several reasons. You may be so reluctant because you think that guilt feelings prevent you from wrongdoing. Actually, they won't. When you experience guilt, you think that you are a bad person. When you think that way about yourself, you are more likely, not less likely, to do bad things. Because that is what bad people do – bad things. Feelings of remorse, on the other hand, are based on the idea that when you do bad things, you are responsible for your actions, but are not a bad person for doing so. Rather, you are a fallible human being, capable of acting well and badly. Feelings of remorse can help you learn why you acted badly and – since you are capable of acting well – can encourage you to use your learning to good effect in the future.

290. Guilt is the enemy of understanding. When you are feeling guilt as opposed to remorse, you condemn yourself as a bad person. This attitude prevents you from reflecting on and understanding your actions. Since you fail to understand why you acted in the way you did, you are likely to act in a similar way again. Thus, guilt increases rather than decreases the likelihood of future wrongdoing.

291. Remorse promotes understanding. When you are feeling remorse as opposed to guilt, you accept yourself unconditionally as a fallible human being. This attitude encourages you to reflect on and understand your actions. Since you understand why you acted in the way you did, you are less likely to act in a similar way again. Thus, remorse decreases rather than increases the likelihood of future wrongdoing.

292. If you consider that you have to feel guilty about a wrongdoing or else you are in danger of becoming psychopathic, you are mistaken. Remorse is not only a healthy alternative to guilt, it also prevents psychopathy.

293. Other people can't make you feel guilty. They only issue you with an invitation for you to make yourself feel guilty. Don't accept this invitation, but take responsibility for any wrongdoing you may have done.

294. Strictly speaking you don't hurt other people's feelings. They hurt their own feelings about the way you treat them. However, this is *not* an excuse for you to act badly, since you are responsible for the way you behave.

295. Are you a parent who, in your heart of hearts, does not love one of your children? Or are you a son or daughter who does not love one or both of your parents? Don't feel guilty. There's no law of the universe that states that you must feel that love. If you accept yourself unconditionally for your lack of these loving feelings, you may be able to identify the reason and do something about it. Condemning yourself will only give you an additional problem. You end up by not loving the other person and hating yourself.

296. When you feel guilty, you focus on your 'sin' and you don't put your behaviour in a wider context. However, when you feel remorseful about your 'sin', you can stand back and place your behaviour in such a context.

297. When you feel guilty about hurting someone's feelings, you are preoccupied with your own badness rather than concerned with how the other person feels.

298. When you feel guilty, your rigid attitude leads you to neglect the context you were in when you acted the way you did. Experiencing guilt-free remorse helps you take this context into account.

299. In addressing your guilt, aim to develop a healthy self-accepting morality, not uncaring psychopathy.

300. Selfishness involves you rigidly pursuing your interests without giving a damn about the interests of others, while self-care involves you flexibly pursuing these interests while sometimes putting the interests of others before your own.

↓

301. If you don't look after yourself, who will?

↓

302. So, self-care is not selfishness and is generally healthy.

↓

303. Selflessness is usually not healthy because it means that you neglect your constructive interests.

304. On a plane, they encourage you to fix your oxygen mask before helping someone to fix theirs. Why?

305. You may think that the only alternative to selfishness is selflessness. If so, you'd be wrong. Enlightened self-interest or self-care is another option and is, in fact, the healthiest of the three positions – since it involves you looking after yourself while being actively mindful of the interests of others.

11

On Regret

306. If you want to overcome unhealthy regret, you first need to understand what leads to this emotion. Unhealthy regret stems in part from the inference that:

- I *took action and chose the wrong path.*
- I *failed to take action and did not choose the right path.*
- I am faced with *making a decision and don't want to regret later what I decide.*

But unhealthy regret really comes from the rigid and extreme attitudes that you hold towards these inferences. Namely:

- I absolutely should not have chosen the path that I did.
- I absolutely should have taken action and chose the path that I did not choose.
- I absolutely must make a decision now which I will not regret later.

307. When you feel unhealthy regret, you will tend to act in the following ways:

- You keep seeking reassurance from others, hoping to be convinced that you had taken the right course of action then but failing to be convinced in the longer term because you are not reassurable.
- You discuss your upcoming decision with others, hoping that they will all recommend you take a particular course of action.

- You will not decide now until you are sure that you will not regret your decision later.

308. When you feel unhealthy regret, you will tend to think in the following ways:

- You are convinced that you took the wrong course of action in the past.
- You think that if you had taken another course of action, your life would have turned out much better.
- You ruminate over past decisions, either hoping to reassure yourself that you did the right thing.
- You ruminate over a present course of action and put off making a decision until you are sure you are making one that you will not regret later.
- You think that there is a perfect solution to making a decision which, if you made, you would never regret your decision.

309. Healthy regret is the healthy alternative to unhealthy regret. In healthy regret, you make the same inferences as in guilt, namely:

- I *took action and chose the wrong path.*
- I *failed to take action and did not choose the right path.*
- I am faced with *making a decision and don't want to regret later what I decide.*

But when you feel healthy regret, you hold a different set of attitudes than when you feel unhealthy regret. These attitudes are flexible and non-extreme in nature. Namely:

- I wished I had not chosen that path that I did, but that doesn't mean that I absolutely should have done so.

- I wish I had taken action and chosen the path that I did not choose, but that doesn't mean that I absolutely should have done so.
- I want to make a decision now which I will not regret later, but I don't have to be successful in this respect.

310. When you feel healthy regret, you will tend to act in the following ways.

- You may tell people about past decisions but not in the hope of getting reassurance from them that you had taken the right course of action.
- You will make a decision now based on what you know at the time and accept the fact that you may or may not regret it later.

311. When you feel healthy regret, you will tend to think in the following realistic and balanced ways:

- You think that you may have taken the wrong course of action, but equally, you may have taken the right one. You acknowledge that there is no way of knowing for certain.
- You think that if you took another course of action, your life may have turned out better, but equally, it may have turned out worse or made no difference to your life.
- You learn from past decisions without ruminating on them.
- You think about a present course of action without ruminating on it. You make the decision in a timely manner, acknowledging that you may or may not regret your decision later.
- You don't think that there is a perfect solution to making a decision and that regret is part of life from which you can learn.

312. Unhealthy regret differs from guilt in that the latter is more concerned with the moral dimension of your life.

313. You cannot live in the past, but you can waste a lot of time in the present thinking about the past.

314. The only productive thing that you can do with past mistakes is to learn from them. Demanding that you absolutely should not have committed these errors in the first place can impede the learning process.

315. When you feel unhealthy regret, you are preoccupied with the rigid attitude that you absolutely should have known then what you know now. But how could you have known this? Do you have a time machine?

316. As with guilt, when you feel unhealthy regret, your rigid attitude leads you to take no notice of the context you were in when you took action or decided not to do so. Experiencing healthy regret helps you to take this context into account.

12

On Anger

317. If you want to overcome unhealthy anger, you first need to understand what leads to this emotion. Unhealthy anger stems in part from the inference that:

- Another has *threatened my self-esteem.*
- Another has *transgressed an important rule* within my personal domain.
- Another has *frustrated your attempts to achieve an important goal* within my personal domain.

But unhealthy anger really comes from the rigid and extreme attitudes that you hold towards these inferences. Namely:

- The other absolutely should not have threatened my self-esteem, transgressed my rule or blocked my path towards my goal.

↓

318. When you feel unhealthy anger, you will tend to act in the following ways.

- You attack the other in some way or feel like doing so.
- You withdraw aggressively.
- You recruit allies against the other.

↓

319. When you feel unhealthy anger, you will tend to think in the following ways:

- You overestimate the extent to which the other acted intentionally and with malice.
- You think about gaining revenge.
- You can't see the other's point of view.
- You think that you are definitely right and the other is definitely wrong.
- You ruminate about the incident and think of how you can come out on top.

320. Healthy anger is the healthy alternative to unhealthy anger. In healthy anger, you make the same inferences as in unhealthy anger, namely:

- Another has *threatened my self-esteem.*
- Another has *transgressed an important rule* within my personal domain.
- Another has *frustrated your attempts to achieve an important goal* within my personal domain.

But when you feel healthy anger, you hold a different set of attitudes than when you feel unhealthy anger. These attitudes are flexible and non-extreme in nature. Namely:

- I really would have preferred it if the other hadn't threatened my self-esteem, transgressed my rule or blocked my path towards my goal; however, sadly and regretfully, they don't have to do what I want.

321. When you feel healthy anger, you will tend to act in the following ways.

- You assert yourself with the other in a respectful manner.
- You stay in the situation and invite the other person to discuss the matter with you.
- You request but do not demand change from the other.

322. When you feel healthy anger, you will tend to think in the following realistic and balanced ways:

- You think that the other may have acted intentionally and with malice but also recognise that this may not be the case.
- You have fleeting but not sustained thoughts of gaining revenge. You don't ruminate about it.
- You can see the other's point of view.
- You think that you are probably, but not definitely right, and the other is probably but not definitely wrong.

323. You may be reluctant to give up your feelings of unhealthy anger for several reasons. You may be so reluctant because you think that your response is justified by the other person's behaviour. Here, it is important to distinguish between the other person's behaviour and your response to it. If the other person has seriously transgressed your personal rules, this is very bad whether you feel unhealthy anger or healthy anger. The behaviour stays the same, but your response is different. Healthy anger enables you to address the transgression without attacking the other person (as in unhealthy anger). It is, in all probability, healthier for you physically (than unhealthy anger), and you are less likely to elicit retaliation from the other person with healthy anger than with unhealthy anger. Healthy anger may be less immediately pleasurable than unhealthy anger, but is a moment of triumph with unhealthy anger worth all of the other negative consequences?

324. To say that someone made you angry is to give them power over your brain. In reality, you make yourself angry over the other person's behaviour by your anger-creating attitudes.

Where do these attitudes reside? In your brain.

Who is largely in control over your brain? You are.

So don't be too quick to hand over this power of control to someone else.

325. It was alleged that Voltaire, the French author, once said to someone: 'I disapprove of what you say, but I will defend to the death your right to say it.' This is a good example of healthy anger. If he had said: 'I disapprove of what you say, and you have no right to say it,' he would have experienced unhealthy anger.

326. Every time you blame others you make it more likely that you will blame yourself in the future,

327. If you really understand someone from their point of view, it is difficult to resent them.

328. We do not question the idea that our enemies are bad, but we do object long and loud when our enemies consider us to be bad.

329. Anger without condemnation is healthy.

330. Martin Luther King Jr. and Gandhi are good role models for healthy anger. Both were angry about injustice, and both were persistent in their ongoing attempts to right wrongs. But neither advocated violence, and both showed that they respected themselves and others.

331. When anger leads to considered, constructive action, it is healthy. When it leads to impulsive, unconstructive action, it is unhealthy.

332. Are you scared of losing control if you express anger? If so, you probably hold one or both of the following two rigid attitudes: (a) I must be in control at all times, and (b) I mustn't feel angry.

333. Once you learn that there is no prohibition on feeling angry and that you don't always have to be in control, then you won't fear losing control while expressing anger, and your anger expression is likely to be focused and respectful but clear.

334. When you experience unhealthy anger, it is worth asking yourself if it is a cover for feelings of hurt, shame or anxiety, for example.

335. If your unhealthy anger is a cover for another unhealthy negative emotion, accept yourself unconditionally for feeling anger and the other emotion and then ask yourself what you feel most disturbed about.

336. Unhealthy anger and its associated behaviours can be an attempt to destroy something or someone that you find very threatening.

337. Ego-defensive anger: The best form of defence is attack.

338. Sometimes, however, unhealthy anger is just plain unhealthy anger.

339. Some forms of unhealthy anger are examples of two-year-old-ism, where you have an attitude: 'Because I want something, I absolutely have to have it, and you have to give it to me.'

340. Other forms of unhealthy anger serve to protect you from threats to your self-esteem. It is as if you are saying: 'You must not remind me how worthless I think I am.'

341. It is popularly believed that when you feel angry, it is important to let it out. I disagree. When your anger is unhealthy, and you let it out, you do two things. First, you practise the rigid attitude that underpins your anger, and second, you may well do harm to the person to whom you express your unhealthy anger.

342. King Canute was unhealthily angry when he demanded that the tide went out on his command. His anger had no effect on the tide, and his feet got wet.

343. Anger is one of the most problematic words in the mental health field since it covers a multitude of sins and graces.

344. Unless you are very clear about the way you are using the term 'anger', then there is a good chance that the person you are talking to will misunderstand you.

345. So, when you are talking about anger there are *four* issues you need to address to determine the nature of this emotion, if the anger is healthy or unhealthy.

346. Issue 1: *What the angry feeling is about.* This will usually be some inferred provocation, breaking a personal new rule or a threat to self-esteem. These occur in both healthy and unhealthy anger.

347. Issue 2: *The attitude that underpins the feeling of anger.* This will be rigid and extreme in unhealthy anger or flexible and non-extreme in healthy anger.

348. Issue 3. *What you did or felt like doing, but didn't do when feeling angry.* Actions that seek to harm the other person indicate unhealthy anger even if these actions are suppressed. If anger-based actions don't seek to harm the other person then they are likely to indicate healthy anger.

↓

349. Issue 4: *The thoughts the person had after the feeling of anger had 'kicked in'.* Thoughts which have a revenge quality to them and are ruminative tend to indicate unhealthy anger.

350. The absence of a feeling of anger in the face of provocation, rule-breaking or self-esteem threat is not normally a constructive response. Since if something bad happens, it is healthy to feel bad about it.

351. I often recommend that people with an anger problem practise Scout therapy: Anticipate the adversity and be prepared to deal with it.

352. Healthy anger is the anger you feel when you are pursuing justice in a determined, non-condemnatory way.

13

On Hurt

353. If you want to overcome hurt, you first need to understand what leads to this emotion. Hurt stems in part from the inference that:

- A significant other in my personal domain has *let me down* and I am *undeserving* of such treatment.
- Another person is *less invested in our relationship than I am*.

But hurt really comes from the rigid and extreme attitudes that you hold towards these inferences. Namely:

- The other absolutely should not let me down as I haven't done anything to deserve it.
- The other person must be as invested in our relationship as I am.

$$\downarrow$$

354. When you feel hurt, you will tend to act in the following ways.

- You shut down the channel of communication between yourself and the other.
- You sulk.
- You wait for the other person to make the first move.

355. When you feel hurt, you will tend to think in the following ways:

- You overestimate the unfairness of the other's behaviour.
- You think that the other person does not care about you.
- You think of yourself as alone, uncared for, and generally misunderstood.
- You tend to think of past hurts.
- You believe in a world where people get what they deserve.

356. Hurt-free sorrow is the healthy alternative to hurt. In sorrow, you make the same inferences as in unhealthy anger, namely:

- Significant others in your personal domain have *let me down,* and I am *undeserving* of such treatment.
- Another person is *less invested in our relationship than I am.*

But when you feel sorrow, you hold a different set of attitudes than when you feel hurt. These attitudes are flexible and non-extreme in nature. Namely:

- I really would have preferred it if the other hadn't let me down but that does not mean that they must not do so even though I am undeserving of such treatment.
- The other person does not have to be as invested in our relationship as I am even though I want them to be.

357. When you feel sorrow, you will tend to act in the following ways.

- You communicate your feelings to the other directly.
- You request, but do not demand, that the other acts in a fairer manner towards you.
- You stay in the situation and invite the other person to discuss the matter with you, and you take responsibility for your contribution to the situation.

358. When you feel sorrow, you will tend to think in the following realistic and balanced ways:

- You are realistic about the degree of unfairness in the other's behaviour.
- You don't equate the other's behaviour towards you as evidence that they do not care about you.
- You think of yourself as being in a poor situation but are still connected to and cared for by others. You think that the other may not understand you, but not that you are generally misunderstood.
- If you think of past hurts, you do so with less frequency and less intensely than when you feel hurt.

359. You may be reluctant to give up your feelings of hurt for several reasons. You may be so reluctant because you think that it is normal to feel hurt when you have been let down. This may be the case, but a 'normal' response is not necessarily a 'healthy' response. The healthy response to hurt is sorrow. Sorrow allows you to come to terms with being let down and encourages you to address this openly with the other person. Hurt, however, will lead you to withdraw from the other, often in an angry and sulky manner. If your goal is to maintain your relationship with people who let you down from time to time (and being human, all people are capable of doing that, including you), then sorrow, rather than hurt, will help you to do so.

360. Hurt may be ego-based or self-pity-based.

361. When you feel hurt-free sorrow, you accept yourself in the face of an imbalanced relationship when you are more invested in your relationship with the other person than they are and/or you regard yourself as being a non-poor person who is in a poor situation.

362. The goal of therapy is to help you feel hurt-free sorrow about another person being less invested in your relationship with them than you are. You do this primarily by changing your attitude towards this adversity.

14

On Jealousy

363. If you want to overcome unhealthy jealousy, you first need to understand what leads to this emotion. Unhealthy jealousy stems in part from the inference that:

- A person poses a threat to a valued relationship within my personal domain (e.g., your partner).
- There is uncertainty in relation to this threat.

But unhealthy jealousy really comes from the rigid and extreme attitudes that you hold towards these inferences. Namely:

- The other person must not pose a threat to my relationship with my partner.
- I must be certain that my valued relationship with my partner is not under threat.

364. When you feel unhealthy jealousy, you will tend to act in the following ways.

- You seek contact reassurance from your partner that the relationship is not under threat and that you are loved, but you doubt their responses.
- You monitor the behaviour of your partner and that of the person who poses a threat to that relationship.
- You search for evidence that your partner is involved with another person.
- You attempt to restrict the movements or activities of your partner.

- You set tests which your partner has to pass.
- You retaliate for your partner's presumed infidelity.
- You sulk.

365. When you feel unhealthy jealousy, you will tend to think in the following ways:

- You exaggerate any threat to your relationship that does exist.
- You think the loss of your relationship is imminent.
- You misconstrue your partner's ordinary conversations with relevant others as having romantic or sexual connotations.
- You construct visual images of your partner's presumed infidelity.
- If your partner admits to finding another person attractive, you think that s/he finds that person more attractive than you and that s/he will leave you for this other person.

366. Healthy jealousy is the healthy alternative to unhealthy jealousy. In healthy jealousy, you make the same inferences as in unhealthy jealousy, namely:

- A person poses a threat to a valued relationship within my personal domain (e.g., your partner).
- There is uncertainty in relation to this threat.

But when you feel healthy jealousy, you hold a different set of attitudes than when you feel unhealthy jealousy. These attitudes are flexible and non-extreme in nature. Namely:

- I don't want the other person to pose a threat to my relationship with my partner, but unfortunately, it doesn't follow that they must not do so.
- I would like to be certain that my valued relationship with my partner is not under threat but I don't need such certainty.

367. When you feel healthy jealousy, you will tend to act in the following ways.

- You allow your partner to initiate expressing love for you without prompting her or seeking reassurance once she has done so.
- You allow your partner freedom without monitoring their feelings, actions and whereabouts.
- You allow your partner to show natural interest in members of the opposite sex without setting tests.
- You communicate your concern for your relationship in an open and non-blaming manner.

368. When you feel healthy jealousy, you will tend to think in the following realistic and balanced ways:

- You tend not to exaggerate any threat to your relationship that does exist.
- You do not misconstrue ordinary conversations between your partner and another person.
- You do not construct visual images of your partner's presumed infidelity.
- You accept that your partner will find others attractive but you do not see this as a threat.

369. You may be reluctant to give up your feelings of unhealthy jealousy for several reasons. You may be so reluctant because you think that it keeps you vigilant for signs of your partner's infidelity, for example. Unhealthy jealousy will certainly keep you vigilant, but it will do so when there is no objective evidence of a threat to your relationship. Indeed, unhealthy jealousy and the rigid and extreme attitudes upon which it is based will lead you to interpret innocuous signs as threats to your relationship. Healthy jealousy and the flexible and non-extreme attitudes upon which it is based will help you to be vigilant when there is a clear threat to your relationship, but it will help you to enjoy that relationship and not contribute to its demise when such a threat is not present. With unhealthy jealousy, you rarely enjoy your relationship because you think that it is constantly under threat, and you may act in ways that put off your significant other. You react this way because you think the threat is *terrible.*

370. In unhealthy jealousy, you are desperate for your partner to reassure you that there is no threat to your relationship. The only problem is that you cannot convince yourself that such reassurance is truly meant if it is given.

371. When you experience unhealthy jealousy, you try to convince yourself of something that you can't be convinced of, but you can't stop trying to convince yourself of it.

372. Unhealthy jealousy is a sure sign of insecurity and low self-esteem. It does not necessarily mean that you are about to lose your loved one.

373. So, the best way to overcome unhealthy jealousy is for you to give up your need for certainty and to accept yourself unconditionally, whether your partner stays with you or not.

374. Many people use the word 'jealous' when they mean 'envious'. This is problematic because they are very different emotions.

375. When you are jealous, you react to a perceived threat to a significant relationship. Thus, jealousy is about losing what you have. When you are envious you react to someone having what you don't have but want. Thus, envy is about not having what you covet.

376. Unhealthy jealousy is not appeased by facts.

377. Why are people who are unhealthily jealous like elephants? Because neither forget.

15

On Envy

378. If you want to overcome unhealthy envy, you first need to understand what leads to this emotion. Unhealthy envy stems in part from the inference that:

- *Another person possesses and/or enjoys something (or someone) which I deem valuable* within my personal domain *which I want but do not have.*

But unhealthy envy really comes from the rigid and extreme attitudes that you hold towards these inferences. Namely:

- I must have what the other has which I want but do not have.

$$\downarrow$$

379. When you feel unhealthy envy, you will tend to act in the following ways.

- You seek what the other has even when it is self-defeating to do so.
- You disparage or try to destroy what the other has.
- If you had the chance you would take away the desired possession from the other (either so that you will have it or that the other is deprived of it).
- If you had the chance you would spoil or destroy the desired possession so that the other person does not have it.

↓

380. When you feel unhealthy envy, you will tend to think in the following ways:

- You tend to denigrate in your mind the value of the desired possession and/or the person who possesses it.
- You try to convince yourself that you are happy with your possessions (although you are not).
- You think about how to acquire the desired possession regardless of its usefulness.
- You think about how to deprive the other person of the desired possession.
- You think about how to spoil or destroy the other's desired possession.
- You think about all the other things the other has that you don't have.

↓

381. Healthy envy is the healthy alternative to unhealthy envy. In healthy envy, you make the same inference as in unhealthy envy, namely:

- *Another person possesses and/or enjoys something (or someone) which I deem valuable within* my personal domain *which I want but do not have.*

But when you feel healthy envy, you hold a different set of attitudes than when you feel unhealthy envy. These attitudes are flexible and non-extreme in nature. Namely:

- I would like to have what the other has, which I want but do not have, but it is not necessary for me to have it.

↓

382. When you feel healthy envy, you will tend to act in the following ways:

- You admit to others that you feel healthily envious.
- You strive to obtain the desired possession if it is truly what you want.

383. When you feel healthy envy, you will tend to think in the following realistic and balanced ways:

- You honestly admit to yourself that you want the desired possession if you truly do.
- You are honest with yourself if you are not happy with your possessions, rather than defensively trying to convince yourself that you are happy with them when you are not.
- You think about how to obtain the desired possession because you want it for healthy reasons.
- You can allow the other person to have and enjoy the desired possession without denigrating that person or the possession.
- You think about what the other has and lacks and what you have and lack.

384. You may be reluctant to give up your feelings of unhealthy envy for several reasons. You may be so reluctant because you think that unhealthy envy motivates you to get what you covet but don't possess. This is partially true, but the obsessive nature of unhealthy envy means that you will pursue what you covet even when doing so is self-destructive. Even if you were to get what you covet, the rigid and extreme attitudes that underpin unhealthy envy will lead you to drop this soon and focus on something else that you covet but don't possess. Literally, you are rarely satisfied when your envy is unhealthy. When your envy is healthy, you will sensibly pursue something that you genuinely want because you want it, not because someone else has it and you don't. When you get what you covet, and your envy is

healthy, then you can enjoy possessing it and not focus on the next coveted object that is in someone else's possession and not yours.

385. A major obstacle to overcoming unhealthy envy is shame about feeling this way.

386. Why do we like to bring down our heroes and heroines? Because we harbour feelings of unhealthy envy towards them.

387. People who feel unhealthy envy are dangerous to have as enemies.

388. When you feel ego-based unhealthy envy, you hold the extreme attitude that gaining something you don't have that another does have will raise your self-esteem if you have it. It will, but only fleetingly.

389. So, the best way to overcome this type of unhealthy envy is to accept yourself unconditionally when you don't have something that you value, which another person has.

390. In a phrase, your worth is not based on what you have or what you lack. If it is based on anything, it is based on your fallibility, your aliveness and your uniqueness.

391. When you feel deprivation-based unhealthy envy, you hold the extreme attitude that you can't bear to be deprived of what you think you must have.

392. The truth is that you can bear it if you choose to. You will be able to do so if you think that it is worth it to you to bear such deprivation and that you are worth bearing it for.

393. Neither form of unhealthy envy is adequately sated in the longer term by gaining your desired possessions. Unhealthy envy is an attitude problem, not a possession problem.

16

On Avoidance and Withdrawal

394. It's no good running away from yourself, for wherever you go, you take yourself with you.

395. When you sweep things under the rug, they have a nasty habit of not going away.

396. Avoiding things will not usually help you to solve your problems. But, if you really want to avoid something, make sure you avoid your avoidance.

397. It is said that humans have descended from the ape, but most of us are descendants of the ostrich, so strong is our tendency to bury our heads in the sand and not face up to dealing with painful issues.

398. If you run away from feelings of discomfort, they will grow and eventually overtake you

17

On Failure

399. Failure is much more interesting than success, for you have much more to learn from failure than you do from success.

400. Experience always teaches you something, but you don't always learn from experience.

401. Success can best be achieved when you have a healthy attitude to failure.

402. Learn the 3 'f's': Failure is evidence of fallibility and provides feedback.

403. Failure is in the doing not in the being.

404. If you really are a failure, then you would have to fail at everything.

405. If you really are a success then you would have to succeed at everything

406. A moment's reflection would tell you, then that there are no failures and successes, just fallible human beings who are capable of success and failure.

18

On Perfectionism

407. You may be able to reach perfection at something, but you cannot maintain it. In 1984, the British figure skaters, Torvill and Dean, achieved a perfect 6.0 for their ice-skating routine at the Winter Olympics. In all probability, however, they wouldn't have done as well if they'd had to skate the same routine again directly afterwards.

408. Salvador Dali urged us to have no fear of perfection since we will never reach it. I would add the words, 'and remain there' since we may temporarily do something perfectly.

409. If you think that you have things perfectly sorted out, then you are deluding yourself or your mind is so closed that it won't let in new information.

410. Here's a thought for those in the legal profession who are scared of making mistakes. While you can resign from the Law Society, you can't resign from the 'Flaw Society'.

411. Thinking that you must be perfect is an error – which proves that you are not perfect.

412. Insisting that you must not make mistakes is a mistake in itself. The healthy alternative is to give up the demand that you must not make errors and learn from them when, not if, you make them.

413. If you haven't made any mistakes lately, you are either dead or playing things extraordinarily safely.

414. Are you a perfectionist? If you ever reached perfection, it would mean that you would be incapable of making a mistake, and you would have nothing else to learn. Since making mistakes and continuing to learn are two fundamental qualities of being human, striving for perfection means striving to be inhuman.

415. Lose the mask of perfection and gain the face of fallibility.

416. Don't say you are prepared to make 110% effort since 100% effort is the most you can make, and given that you are human, you often won't do so.

417. What do people say that they are a 'bit' of a perfectionist? Why not a 'lot' of a perfectionist?

418. As the noted psychiatrist Maxie C. Maultsby once said: As a human, you have an incurable error-making tendency.

19

On Uncertainty and Making Decisions

419. A donkey was dying of thirst in the desert and came to a fork in the road. It knew that one path led to clear water while the other led to dank water that would save its life but make it ill. But the donkey did not know which path led to which type of water. The donkey died. Why? Because it held the rigid attitude that it had to know which road led to the clear water before it set out.

420. When you are indecisive and finally make a decision, you automatically tend to think that your decision is wrong and that the other option which you decided against would have been correct. You tend to think in this way no matter what course of action you finally decide on.

421. Once you have made a decision, it is no good demanding that you absolutely should have done something different, for you empirically should have done exactly what you did. If you accept this, you will move forward. If you don't accept it, you will be stuck in the past.

422. If you think about it, it is not possible to be indecisive. Because when you do nothing, you are actively deciding to do nothing.

423. Some people are anything but indecisive. They are impulsive in their decision-making. They see an attractive option and immediately decide to go for it. When you are indecisive, you hold the rigid attitude that you must not make a mistake but are convinced that you will. When you are impulsive, you hold the rigid attitude that you must have what you want right now and are convinced that you are doing the right thing.

424. When you are indecisive, you think too much, whereas when you are impulsive in your decision-making, you think too little.

425. To make a sound decision, it is important that you are in an emotionally good frame of mind. Otherwise, your disturbed emotions will cloud your judgement.

$$\downarrow$$

426. Once you are in a good frame of mind, what do you need to do to increase the chances that you will make a sound decision? I suggest the following. Consider the pros and cons of your different options from both a short-term and a long-term perspective as they relate to yourself (and your values in particular) and to relevant others. If you do this rigorously (rather than rigidly!), your preferred option will, in all probability, become much clearer to you.

427. Accepting and acting on probability is the antidote to dealing with demands for certainty.

428. When you think you need to know what will happen later, you cheat life of its process.

429. The goal is not to remove all doubts, but to tackle your rigidity about the doubts.

430. People tend only to be anxious about uncertainty when this uncertainty relates to some other threat (e.g., ill health or loss of self-control).

431. Our attempts to gain certainty with respect to a threat will often perpetuate our uncertainty-based anxiety, especially when these attempts are desperate. Instead, we need to bear uncertainty before we try to reduce it.

432. Seeking reassurance once or twice over something is fine. But if you are not reassured, it is futile to keep seeking reassurance since you are not reassurable.

433. If you seek reassurance compulsively, look for the rigid attitude that underpins your behaviour. It is likely to be: 'I must be certain right now that nothing bad is happening (or is likely to happen) to me.' It is important to change this attitude to: 'I would like to have such certainty, but I don't need it, nor can I get it.' Then it is important to act in a way that is consistent with this attitude. Giving up the dire need for certainty will allow you to live healthily in an uncertain world.

434. Reassurances like candy floss. It is sweet but without substance. You eat it, and you are quickly dissatisfied.

435. See doubt as a green light, not as a red light.

20

On Procrastination

436. If you are going to tackle your procrastination, start today.

437. There are four basic reasons why people procrastinate on tasks that are in their best interests to do:

- Fear of failure
- Fear of disappointing others
- Fear of discomfort
- Rebellion.

438. Putting off doing something that is it not in your best interests to do is not procrastination. It is sensible.

439. People often ask me how I manage to write so much. The answer is discipline. When I am in a writing phase, I resolve to write 500 words a day every day. 'But,' they ask, 'what if you are not in the mood?' My answer is this: 'If I'm not in the mood, I start writing anyway, and nine times out of ten, I get in the mood.' So, if you want to do something and are not in the mood, don't let that stop you. Begin anyway. Chances are that, like me, you'll soon get into the mood. You don't need to be in the mood to do something.

440. Don't wait for inspiration to come before you do something. Do something, and inspiration may come; do nothing, and it's unlikely to.

441. If you wait until you feel like doing something onerous that is in your best interest, you will wait too long.

442. If you leave things until the last minute, you may motivate yourself but in an unduly pressurised way.

443. When you procrastinate, ask yourself the following question: 'What conditions do I think I need to be in place for me to start the task that I am procrastinating over?'

444. Then, ask yourself: 'Is this condition really necessary or is it possible for me to start work without it?' You will find that the latter is almost always the case.

445. So, train yourself to start work even if you don't have the desired condition in place. This involves you going against the grain. The more you do so, the more you will develop a new grain that you will be going with, not against.

446. Procrastination is generally self-defeating. Why? I'll tell you tomorrow!

447. The thing you should put off until tomorrow is putting off things until tomorrow.

448. When people talk about motivation, it is important to discover as precisely as possible what they mean by this term.

449. Sometimes they mean by being motivated that they have a good reason to do something.

450. Other times they're referring to a feeling state as in 'feeling motivated' to do something.

451. While it may be best to have both reason-based and feeling-based motivation, the former is generally more productive in the long term than the latter.

452. If you believe that you can do something that you have a good reason to do without feeling like you want to do it, then you will help yourself far more in the long term than if you are all fired up to do something you really don't have a good reason to do.

21

On Self-Discipline

453. Eating, drinking or spending to avoid disturbed feelings won't help you to deal with these feelings. However, doing so may help to set the foundations for an addiction.

454. Giving up smoking does not involve the application of willpower. It involves the application of won't power and following several simple steps.

$$\downarrow$$

455. The first step to giving up smoking is to be very clear with yourself about why you want to give up. Remind yourself of your goal every time you experience an urge to light up.

$$\downarrow$$

456. The second step is to stop buying cigarettes. It's amazing how many people violate this simple rule.

$$\downarrow$$

457. The third step is not to accept cigarettes when they are offered to you.

$$\downarrow$$

458. The fourth step involves tolerating the discomfort that you experience when you say no to yourself when you crave a cigarette.

↓

459. The fifth step involves seeking out and spending time in non-smoking areas and spending time with people who don't smoke. Then, when you feel stronger, gradually expose yourself to smoking environments and don't smoke in them.

460. I do a brisk jog-walk for 50 minutes six mornings a week, and frequently, I don't want to do it. But I do so anyway. Why? Because it helps me to stay fit in the long term.

461. Persistence is a virtue if the activity you are persisting in helps you achieve your goals. However, persisting with an activity that does not enhance good achievement is counterproductive.

462. Discipline involves you doing something that you don't want to do in order to get the results that you do want.

463. You are not lazy, but you may hold the extreme attitude that it's too hard to do something that is unpleasant but worth doing. You can change this attitude more easily than you could change your supposed inherent laziness.

464. Lists are fine if they promote constructive action.

465. If you want to lose weight, you need FAT: (i) *F*rustration tolerance, (ii) *A*cceptance; and (iii) *T*enacity.

466. Misuse of alcohol = a quick fix to deal with a problem that cannot be fixed quickly.

467. Absence may make the heart grow stronger, but abstinence makes the liver grow stronger.

468. Remind yourself of the seven main principles of self-discipline:

- 'It's difficult to do.'
- 'I can bear doing it.'
- 'It's worth doing.'
- 'I'm worth doing it for.'
- 'I'm willing to do what it takes.'
- 'I commit myself to doing it.'
- 'I make it harder for myself if I don't do it.'

22

On Responsibility and Control

469. Life is like a game of cards. It's not so much the cards you are dealt that are important but how you choose to play them.

470. People are reluctant to take responsibility because they confuse responsibility with blame. Responsibility is, 'I did it with my little hatchet, but I am not a bad person for doing so.' This attitude will help you to understand why you acted in the way that you did and help to prevent you from acting that way again.

Blame, on the other hand, is, 'I did it with my little hatchet, and I am a bad person for doing so.' This attitude will prevent you from understanding the reasons for your behaviour and will, therefore, not prevent its recurrence.

So, take responsibility for your actions without blaming yourself for them.

471. People are influenced by what is in their heads, not by what is in yours.

472. Have you ever said that you couldn't help yourself when you ate that cream cake which spoiled your diet? Of course, you couldn't help yourself. After all, the cream cake literally rose off the plate on its own, prised your lips apart and rammed itself down your throat.

Or perhaps it would be wise to take responsibility for your actions instead. Either that or beware of low-flying cream cakes!

473. When you feel disturbed, remember that your thoughts are more likely to reflect your problem than a guide to reality.

474. Nobody can break your heart. They can treat you badly, cheat on you, betray you and otherwise muck you around. But break your heart? No! Only you can disturb yourself about all these negative behaviours from others. However, even if your heart can be broken, you can mend it by un-disturbing yourself about these adversities.

475. Asking for something is in your control. Receiving it isn't.

476. You are the author of your own attitude of unconditional self-acceptance.

477. Nobody can control you by pressing your buttons. First, you don't have any buttons, and second, if you did, you would be the one pressing them.

478. Sticks and stones may break your bones, but names can never hurt you unless you apply them to yourself.

479. True control is based on flexibility.

480. Gain control by letting it happen rather than by making it happen.

481. Healthy self-control = Accepting and allowing experience
    Unhealthy self-control = Rejecting and attempting to eliminate experience.

23

On Relationships with Others

482. When you buy a product like a washing machine or a refrigerator, it comes with a user manual which shows you how to get the best from your product. It is useful to think that every person has a user manual, which, if you knew about, would help you to get the best out of them for their benefit and for the relationship that you have with them.

↓

483. Unfortunately, a person's user manual is not written down anywhere, so you need to discover what this is with active help from the person.

↓

484. You need to help them learn about your user manual so that they can help you to get the best from yourself for your benefit and for the relationship that they have with you.

485. When you do something kind for others, most of them will do something kind for you. However, others will exploit your kindness. Don't hold the rigid attitude that everyone must reciprocate your behaviour because they won't.

486. When people reciprocate your kindness, continue being kind to them. When they take advantage of your kindness, stop being kind to them.

487. If you want someone to listen to you, listen to them first.

488. You cannot change others, but you can influence them to change themselves.

489. However, accept the grim reality that they will often decide not to change.

490. People will often pay more attention to your behaviour than to your words.

491. It is not a good idea to treat all people the same because all people are not the same.

492. People will be who they are, not who you demand them to be.

493. If you show others respect, then they will show you respect. But not always.

494. If you want people to respect you, show them by your behaviour that you respect yourself.

495. Other people's emotional problems will often interfere with their ability to listen to reason.

496. If you want to gauge a person's real attitude, watch their behaviour; don't just listen to their words.

497. People often spend too much time trying to change others and not enough time trying to change themselves.

498. If you want someone to change their behaviour towards you, change your behaviour towards them first.

499. When you argue with someone you probably hold the rigid attitude that the other person has to see things from your point of view. When you flexibly allow the person in your mind to see things from their point of view and not yours, you are less likely to argue with them.

500. If you hold the rigid attitude that you must have approval from people and are prepared to change yourself to get it, don't be surprised if you end up not knowing who you are.

501. If you ever became perfect, you would be lonely. Why? Because we tend to shy away from having a relationship with someone without any imperfections. Who wants to be reminded at every turn of how imperfect we are?

502. Treat people as though they are bad and you will increase the chances that they will act badly.

503. If you only listen to others and not to yourself, then you may feel comfortable but you will be out of step with yourself. If you only listen to yourself and not to others, then you will be clear but be out of step with others. But if you listen to yourself *and* to others, you will be in step with yourself and with others.

504. Trying to influence someone for their own good may not be for their own good.

505. Honour your commitments to others, and they will tend to honour their commitments to you. Note the word 'tend' here. For some people will not respond in kind.

506. Showing that you understand someone from their standpoint is good for both of you and for your relationship.

507. If you want to understand someone's behaviour, try to figure out what the person was attempting to achieve by it.

508. If you hold the rigid attitude that you need to help people, you will probably have relationships with people who need to be helped. If you help them to stand on their own two feet, then expect them to leave you because they don't need you anymore.

509. If someone treats you badly, show them that you will not put up with being treated in this way and demonstrate this immediately. The longer you wait, the more likely it is that the other person will continue to treat you badly.

510. If you don't look after yourself, who will? Only someone who holds the rigid attitude that they need to look after people, and you won't want a relationship with such a person in the long term.

511. Having a relationship with a person who holds the rigid attitude that they need you is ultimately unhealthy for both of you.

512. Showing your loved ones that you accept them warts and all and that you want them to be themselves is one of the two main keys to excellent relationships. Encouraging them to do the same for you is the other key.

513. Love does not mean putting up with bad behaviour from those you love.

514. People who hold the rigid attitude that they need people are the unluckiest people in the world. Why? Because of their neediness.

515. People who hold the flexible attitude that they very much prefer to have people in their life but do not need them are the healthiest people in the world.

516. If you hold the rigid attitude that you need to be needed, you cannot have a healthy relationship because you will tend to be only involved with those who are psychologically immature.

517. When we show others that we can be vulnerable, most of them will be prepared to show us their vulnerabilities. But others, a minority fortunately, will seek to exploit our vulnerabilities for their own disturbed gains.

518. If someone with whom you want a relationship does not want a relationship with you, that is both bad and good. It's bad because your desire will not be fulfilled, but it's good because you won't waste time trying to develop a relationship with someone who is not for you.

519. If someone does not want a relationship with you, let them go. Trying to get them to change their mind will only sour relations between the two of you.

520. Being dependent upon someone means not using your own resources.

521. If you only give in a relationship, you will probably end up resenting the fact that the other person only takes. Don't be resentful, since without realising if you have trained the other person to expect to take from you and not to give back.

522. If you only take in a relationship, you will probably end up being alone.

523. A healthy relationship is marked by the willingness of both people to give and receive.

524. If you allow others to dominate you, most will.

525. If you cannot be at ease with yourself when you are by yourself, then you will find it difficult to be at ease with others, for holding the rigid attitude that you need to be with others to avoid the horrors of being alone will make you scared that they will leave you. Overcoming the horrors of being alone will help you be at ease with others and by yourself.

526. The best way to get closer to someone when you feel detached from them is to talk to them about your feelings of detachment from them.

527. A problem with your partner? Be aware that you can't change them, but you can exchange them! However, you may end up with the same problem with the new partner. For the problem might be you and not them.

528. If you have a long list of requirements for a partner, you may end up alone.

529. A person would often rather have presence from their loved one than presents from their loved one.

530. We spend more time surveying potential houses than potential spouses.

531. All people bring baggage to a relationship. The trick is not to pick someone who has exceeded the weight limit. Otherwise, you will end up paying for their excess baggage.

532. Treat others as you would want them to treat your loved ones.

533. Care about the opinions of the people you care about, not about the opinions of those you don't.

534. Trust is based on the foundation of behaviour, not on the shifting sands of words.

535. If you disturb yourself about others, you may find doing the following helpful. First, identify the possible rigid and extreme attitudes held by these people. Then, reflect on this: these people are driven to behave badly by their unhealthy attitudes. This may help you surrender your own demands that such people must not act badly.

536. Make sure you have the other person's full attention before you assert yourself with them.

537. Once you have learned to assert yourself, you have acquired a very valuable tool. But don't think that everyone with whom you assert yourself will listen attentively to you and give you your just desserts. Some will, but others won't. So, if you believe that people have to take you seriously when you assert yourself, you will disturb yourself when they don't. Rather, cultivate the flexible attitude that it would be nice if others took you seriously when you asserted yourself, but they are not obligated to do so.

24

On Assertion

538. Asserting yourself is healthy, but it doesn't mean that you will get what you want, no matter how skilfully you do it.

539. There are many situations to complain about. If you let them all go, you will tend to feel powerless, and if you complain about them all, you will tend to feel angry and exhausted. Be selective, and when you have made your choice, be persistent, firm and fight fair.

540. You are likely to get obnoxious behaviour from others when you put up with this behaviour and don't actively protest against it. Identify and deal with your obstacles to making such protests, and then make them.

541. Honesty is important but needs to be expressed with due regard to the recipient of your honesty.

542. Sometimes, keeping quiet is the best thing you can do.

543. Sometimes, speaking up is the best thing you can do.

544. There is no magic formula for knowing when to speak up and when to keep quiet.

545. While speaking your mind may be better for you than suppressing your feelings, it may get you into trouble with other people.

546. Thus, before you assert yourself with someone, think carefully about the impact that your assertion is likely to have on the other person before you decide to speak up.

547. However, you may decide that speaking your mind is so important that you will do it no matter what the impact is. If so, then speak your mind and accept the consequences.

548. Assertion involves standing up to be counted in front of people who may discount you.

549. If you do not teach others where your boundaries lie, then these people are likely to cross them and keep crossing them. If you are stopping yourself from setting boundaries with others, look for the implicit rigid demands you are making about yourself and others that lie at the core of your failure to assert your healthy boundaries, For example, rigidly demanding that others must always approve of you will stop you from healthily asserting yourself. If you find such rigid demands, examine and change them – and act on your non-dogmatic, flexible preferences by asserting yourself.

550. When you rigidly demand that you mustn't have problems, doing so doesn't get rid of these problems; it multiplies them.

25

On Parents

551. Just because your parents are your parents, it doesn't follow that they have to love you. Why? Because your parents are human first and your parents second, being human means that their emotional problems may interfere with them loving you.

552. Also, there is no law of the universe which decrees that you have to love your parents.

553. Your parents influence you as you grow up and teach you various standards. But you bring your own rigid attitude to those standards and it is this rigidity, not your failure to live up to those standards, which are at the core of your emotional problems.

554. If your parents mistreated you, they probably did so because of their own emotional problems. This is not meant to excuse your parents but to help you understand why they may have acted in the way that they did.

555. Your parents may say that you will always be their little boy or little girl. But this does not mean you must act like one with them.

556. The only way to prove to your parents that you are an adult is to act like an adult with them and to do so consistently. After a while, they'll probably get the message.

↓

557. However, some parents never get the message.

↓

558. If they don't, remember that they will view you how they choose to view you and not how you want to be viewed.

559. Encourage your adult children to do what is in their best interests, not what is in yours. But who decides what is in their best interests? If you think that you do, then you have a problem letting your adult children be adults.

560. Parents who show their children that they respect themselves and that they have time for themselves as well as time for their children serve as good role models for their children.

561. Parents who put themselves last all the time, and who show their children that they don't have time for themselves and only time for their children, serve as poor role models and doormats for their children.

562. You didn't choose your biological parents. But remember, your biological parents didn't choose you, either.

563. Insisting that you are nothing like your parents will lead you to over-emphasise your similarity with them.

26

On Being Human

564. All humans are capable of the greatest good and the worst evil.

↓

565. However, because we cannot accept this, we locate badness in others, thus preserving the myth that we are good.

566. When you disturb yourself about a disturbance, it is like being in a fight where you are hit and you hit yourself.

567. In one sense, humans need adversity because we cannot build up our psychological immune system if we aren't exposed to adversity. It's the same with physical health. If we aren't introduced to germs, we can't build up our physical immune system.

568. A person cannot realistically be expected to hold a non-judgemental attitude towards a negative thought, feeling or experience for too long.

569. Adversity offers us an opportunity to grow. Without it, we will stagnate.

570. If you need inspiration to overcome great tragedy, you might find this quote from Viktor Frankl useful:

'We who lived in concentration camps can remember the men who walked through the huts comforting others, giving away their last piece of bread. They may have been small in number, but they offer sufficient proof that everything can be taken

away from a man but one thing: the last of human freedoms –
to choose one's attitude in any given set of circumstances, to
choose one's way.'

571. Don't be afraid to admit that you don't know something.
This means that you are a person who does not know something.
It does not mean that you are an ignorant person. With this
attitude, owning up to your ignorance will spur you to find out
the answer to what you don't know.

572. Admitting ignorance is a prerequisite to learning.

573. Are you too proud to admit that you are wrong? This is not
pride. It is a refusal to accept your humanity. By all means, be
proud, but be proud of being human. This will help you to admit
your mistakes and to move forward.

27

On Critical Thinking

574. Just because you look up to someone doesn't mean that they're always right. Think critically about what your idols say.

575. Experts are worth listening to, but they are not infallible. They also may not know your individual situation. So don't use the thinking of experts as a substitute for your own thinking.

576. Pedestals are for statues, not humans.

577. If someone gives you advice, don't automatically assume that it is right and don't automatically assume that it is wrong. Evaluate the advice carefully and take it if it makes sense to you.

578. Two phrases are characteristic of a healthy, inquiring mind. They are: 'I don't know,' and 'I'll find out.'

579. To admit that you were wrong after being convinced that you were right is a mark of great maturity.

580. A hundred people chanting a falsehood does not make it true.

581. Thinking for yourself – one of the great gifts of being human.

582. Letting others do your thinking for you – one of the great follies of being human.

583. It is important that you guard against emotional reasoning, where you believe that something is true because you strongly feel that it is true (e.g., 'Because I strongly feel in my gut that my girlfriend is seeing someone else, therefore she is'). Just because you have a strong feeling, it doesn't follow that this feeling is necessarily a good guide to reality. It may be, but it doesn't have to be, so test your strong feelings against reality.

584. Similarly, it is important to guard against cognitive reasoning, where you are sure that something is true because you think it is true (e.g., 'Because I think that people are following me, this proves that they are'). For obvious reasons, it is important to test such thoughts against reality.

585. Don't be dazzled by complicated rhetoric. Just because something sounds profound doesn't mean that it is profound.

586. Don't dismiss simple ideas. Just because something sounds simple doesn't mean that it is simplistic.

587. How can you tell if what you think you want is really what you want or what others want for you? Imagine that others want you to do the opposite. If you are prepared to change to meet their expectations, your original desire is not what *you* really want.

588. Just because something is new doesn't mean that it is better than the old.

589. Don't follow maxims slavishly and unthinkingly – even this one.

590. A defining feature of psychological health is being able to think for yourself. Thus, I would be happier for you to think critically about what I have written in this book and to conclude that I am wrong than I would be for you to accept uncritically what I have written as being correct.

591. It is important for you to hold onto your mantra while others are chanting theirs.

592. A falsehood is not rendered true by emphasis and/or repetition.

593. Don't accept something as true because an authority has said it, even if that authority is your therapist. Use your brain, not theirs.

28

On Personal Change

594. It is important that you understand the difference between intellectual insight and emotional insight if your personal change is to be meaningful.

↓

595. Intellectual insight involves seeing that something makes sense but only having a slight conviction in it. This type of insight is insufficient to lead to meaningful emotional and behavioural change. It is summed up in statements such as, 'I can see it in my head, but I don't feel it in my gut.'

↓

596. Emotional insight involves seeing that something makes sense and having a strong conviction in it. This type of insight does lead to meaningful emotional and behavioural change. It is summed up in statements such as, 'I both see it in my head and feel it in my gut.'

↓

597. Meaningful personal change, therefore, involves moving from intellectual insight to emotional insight. This is easier said than done, but the good news is that you can make the journey.

598. However, most people won't make this journey because they hold the extreme attitude that it is too hard. The journey is hard, but in reality, it isn't *too* hard.

599. Others won't make the journey because they hold the rigid attitude that they absolutely shouldn't have to make the journey and that they must get emotional insight immediately, and if they don't, then they won't work towards achieving it.

600. It is important that you acknowledge that personal change involves feeling uncomfortable. Holding the rigid attitude that you must be comfortable while you change is a sure way of stopping yourself from changing.

601. When you commit yourself to personal change, it is important to realise that sometimes you will take two steps forward and one step back, and at other times, you will take one step forward and two steps back. The important thing is to learn from your setbacks and keep moving forward.

602. Don't expect to change a deeply held unhealthy attitude quickly. To change such an attitude, you need first to understand what the healthy alternative to this attitude is and then to commit yourself to it.

603. Next, you need to understand why your unhealthy attitude is unhealthy and why the healthy alternative is healthy.

604. An important part of a personal change programme involves weakening your conviction in your rigid and extreme attitudes and strengthening your conviction in your flexible and non-extreme attitudes.

605. But perhaps the most important part of a personal change programme is acting on your newly acquired flexible and non-extreme attitudes. Unless you act on these attitudes, you will not internalise them, and they will not make a difference in your everyday life.

606. You need to persist with such actions and thinking until your feelings change.

607. As you do this, it is important that you accept that your initial response to an adversity may stem from your rigid and extreme attitude.

608. If you accept this, then you can make the appropriate response and resume the process of change.

609. If you don't accept this, then you may disturb yourself about your initial response and go back to your rigid/extreme attitude.

610. One of the best ways to strengthen your conviction in a flexible and non-extreme attitude that makes sense to you, and you wish to adopt is to act *as if* you already hold it.

611. How much time do you spend every day maintaining your physical well-being? You'd be surprised how much time you spend on washing yourself, cleaning yourself, feeding yourself, and on exercising, etc.

If you were to spend half this time every day maintaining your psychological well-being, you would be pleasantly surprised at the difference this would make to your life.

612. Changing unwanted personal habits takes hard work and persistence. If anyone tells you otherwise and promises you a quick and easy way to achieve your goals, they probably want to get rich at your expense.

613. When you begin to change, it won't feel natural. It's not supposed to. So, as you change accept the fact that you won't feel like yourself for a while.

614. It is important to distinguish between feeling better and getting better. Feeling better without getting better involves a temporary distraction from what you are disturbed about. Getting better and not feeling better occurs when you begin to address your emotional problems in a constructive way, a process which is painful. Getting better and feeling better occurs when you have successfully overcome your problems.

615. Most people want to feel better than to get better because they want a painless solution to their emotional problems which largely does not exist.

616. So, if you want to get better realise that this involves you bearing a period of not feeling better, and in some cases a period of feeling worse, as you confront and deal with painful issues that you may have partly avoided.

617. In order to change, it is important to acknowledge that this involves you regularly changing the way you behave and the way that you think *before* your feelings begin to change. Feelings are slow starters when it comes to the change process.

618. If you are going to change, it is vital that your actions are consistent with your flexible and non-extreme attitudes. It is no good thinking one way and acting in a way that is inconsistent with these attitudes. You will just undermine the change process if you do so.

619. Starve your unhealthy attitudes of oxygen by not acting on them. Instead oxygenate your healthy attitudes by relevant constructive action.

620. Change involves noticing small signs of progress and building on them.

621. Ignoring small signs of progress and focusing on the gap between where you are and where you want to be will block your progress.

622. Do you hold the rigid attitude that personal changes be quick, painless and effortless? Then you won't change at all.

623. Half-hearted action will yield moderate results.

624. Committed action will yield far better results.

625. Practice makes better, not perfect.

626. Thought without action may be interesting, but it is theoretical. Action without thought may be exciting but it is potentially dangerous. Thoughtful action is the best of both worlds.

627. 'I'll try' comes before 'I didn't'.

628. Trying to do something is far less effective than doing it.

629. Confidence comes from doing things unconfidently and learning along the way.

630. Confidence is like the back end of a pantomime horse. It comes later.

631. Don't put the cart of confidence before the horse of action.

632. Here are three approaches to personal change. Which approach would you choose?

Approach 1: Opting to feel better but getting worse
Approach 2: Opting to feel worse before getting better
Approach 3: Opting to feel better before getting better.

Number 2 is the only realistic approach to personal change. If you opt for number 3 you will have a very long wait.

633. If something seems too difficult, break it down into smaller steps.

634. If at first you don't succeed, try the same thing twice more. Then consider the possibility that what you are doing won't yield the results that you are striving for.

635. Working hard at something strengthens your psychological muscles for working hard.

636. Reading self-help books won't help you to solve your problems. Repeatedly putting into practice what you read in such books may do so.

637. Knowing when to respond to rigid and extreme thinking and when to accept it mindfully is core to the process of change.

638. Respond to your unconstructive thinking but once you get tangled up in such thinking it is time to stop responding to it and time to start mindfully accepting it.

639. People are more likely to change their minds if they find arguments to do so persuasive rather than true or logical.

640. 'Going against the grain' is perhaps one of the most important skills when initiating and maintaining psychological change.

641. Sometimes the best counter to unconstructive thinking is constructive action.

642. If it doesn't feel strange, it probably isn't change.

643. The road from understanding a flexible and non-extreme attitude in your head to believing it in your gut is paved with hard work.

644. There is no comfortable way to step out of your comfort zone.

645. During the process of change, you may experience some doubts, reservations or objections (DROs) to adopting a flexible/non-extreme attitude and/or giving up the alternative rigid/extreme. Accept this as a natural part of the change process and respond convincingly to these DROs.

646. Dealing constructively with urges to act in ways that bring relief or satisfaction/pleasure in the short-term but that are unhealthy for the person in the long-term is one of the most important but difficult tasks in the change process.

647. Learning to avoid dealing with such urges in unconstructive ways is an important first step. Let me outline the four major ways in which people deal with urges unconstructively so you can avoid them using them.

↓

648. 1: *Act on the urge.* If you act on it you satisfy it but strengthen it in the longer term.

↓

649. 2: *Avoid situations in which you experience the urge.* This does not help you to face the urge and learn to deal with it constructively.

↓

650. 3: *Distract yourself from the urge.* This does not help you to face and deal with the urge.

↓

651. 4: *Engage in another pleasurable, but less harmful behaviour.* This is known as harm reduction and while it again does not help you to deal with the original urge, it leads to less troublesome results.

↓

652. Learning to deal with such urges in constructive ways is the next step. Let me outline the three major ways in which people deal with urges constructively So you can make use of them.

↓

653. 1: *Acknowledge the existence of the urge and realise that you don't have to act on it.* You have choices.

↓

654. 2: *Stay with the urge and don't act on it or do anything to modify it.* If you stay with the urge then it will eventually go, perhaps after initially increasing in intensity when you don't act on it.

↓

655. 3: *Act in ways that are consistent with your longer-term goals and your values.* Doing so will help you to see the horizon beyond the urge and take steps to move towards this horizon.

656. Developing an attitude of unconditional self-acceptance (USA) is like planting seeds. You need to water and feed the seeds and realise that nothing will happen for a while. Constructive action is the water and rehearsing the USA attitude is the plant food.

657. Change is like walking up a hill with a strong wind blowing into your face.

658. In order to use the skills of any therapy when you need them, you need to practise them when you don't.

659. How you respond to a disturbed reaction is more important than the reaction itself.

660. You don't retrain your brain without the active help of your behaviour.

661. Complacency is the mother of relapse.

662. A caterpillar turning into a butterfly is not a good metaphor for personal change for such change rarely happens overnight.

663. Early intervention is better than later remediation.

664. If you have the time to disturb yourself, you have the time to undisturb yourself.

665. Holding on to a flexible attitude under pressure is like holding onto an open umbrella in a strong wind. You can do it but you need to do so skilfully and such skill requires much practice.

666. Understanding is the first step towards change, not the last step.

667. Challenging inferences without changing attitudes first is like trying to burst bubbles without first disabling the bubble-making machine.

668. Awfulising is not cured by experience. It is best responded to by de-awfulising.

669. A trip to 'horror' seems like a one-way trip. Not so, you can always come back from 'horror' if you develop a non-horror attitude.

670. Just because something is difficult does not mean that you can't do it. It means that you can do it, with difficulty.

671. Discomfort is your friend and not your enemy when it comes to personal change.

672. Regular behaviour based on flexible and non-extreme attitudes is the bridge between intellectual insight and emotional insight.

673. Reading self-help books without taking action is like reading travel guides without visiting the places concerned. All knowledge and no experience.

674. Your default position may be faulty, but you can change it when it occurs.

675. De-mustify your rigid mind.

676. The easy option in the short-term is not the easy option in the long-term.

677. Develop healthy attitudes not platitudes.

678. Aim to apply any therapy program flexibly and not rigidly.

679. How best to learn from failure? Realise that from the ashes of disaster grow the roses of success (from 'The Roses of Success' in the film *Chitty Chitty Bang Bang*).

680. From a therapeutic point of view your enemies are more helpful to you than your friends. Your friends will reassure you and tell you that you are great. This is fine, but it won't help you deal with adversity. Your enemies, however, will provide you with plenty of opportunities to deal effectively with adversity. So mix with your friends, but also seek out your enemies.

681. Knowing when to take action to change an adversity is an important skill, but not one you can develop to perfection.

682. Persistence will pay off especially if you are persistently working towards valued goals.

683. An inspiring idea which is not implemented with persistence is like a firework: flashy, but short-lived.

684. Before taking action, listen to what others have to say while taking into account their biases. Then, act in your best interests.

685. Before taking action, listen to what you have to say while taking into account your biases. Then act in your best interests.

686. Balancing your short-term and long-term interests before taking action is a skill that requires ongoing refinement.

687. A girl with learning difficulties wanted to go to China on a Nordic walking holiday but had to prove her fitness first. Every time she was reluctant to go training, she just said 'China' and went.

$$\downarrow$$

688. Figure out what your 'China' is and use it to encourage yourself to do what you are reluctant to do but which is in your best interests to do.

689. Unless you have a clear goal in mind it is unlikely that you will sustain purposeful activity.

690. If you don't face reality, reality will eventually face you.

691. Answer the following questions:

   a. Do you want to improve very quickly, at a moderate speed, or slowly?
   b. Do you want to exert much effort, moderate effort, or little effort while helping yourself to change?

If you want to improve very quickly while expending little effort, you are looking for magic.

In general, the speed of your improvement is proportional to the amount of effort you are prepared to devote to self-help.

692. The more you tend to disturb yourself in certain areas, the harder you need to work to undisturb yourself in these areas.

693. Before facing an adversity in reality, you might find it helpful to first do so in your imagination. As you do so, challenge your rigid and extreme attitudes and rehearse the alternative flexible and non-extreme attitudes.

694. When facing adversities, it is useful to rehearse your flexible and non-extreme attitudes before, during and after such encounters.

695. When facing these adversities, it is important that you do not engage in any safety-seeking behaviours that interfere with this 'facing' process.

696. Understand how you maintain your specific and core rigid and extreme attitudes. You do this by:

- Thinking, feeling, and acting in ways that maintain these attitudes;
- Inappropriately avoiding situations in which you are likely to activate these attitudes; and
- Over-compensating for these attitudes by pretending that you do not hold them, and even thinking that you hold the opposite, flexible and non-extreme attitudes.

697. These maintenance factors feel familiar. Not engaging in them may feel strange. Allow yourself to feel strange as you keep working for change. Eventually, the change will feel familiar.

698. Therapeutic change is non-linear. You may take one step backward for every two that you take forward. Indeed, you may even take two steps backward and one forward. If you remind yourself of this and digest it, you won't become discouraged when you experience setbacks.

699. Maintaining psychological well-being involves taking regular psychological exercise, in the same way that maintaining physical well-being involves taking regular physical exercise.

700. Monitor your improvement by employing three criteria:

- Frequency – do you experience your problems less frequently than before?
- Intensity – are your problems less severe/intense than before?
- Duration – do your problems last for shorter periods than before?

701. Once you have gotten better, you still have to work to stay better.

702. In order to make and maintain your therapeutic gains, you need to recognise and **act** upon the following:

- You make yourself disturbed by the rigid and extreme attitudes you hold towards adversity.
- You can undisturb yourself by examining and changing your rigid and extreme attitudes to flexible and non-extreme attitudes.
- You need to continue this process strongly and steadily over time.

703. You may hinder your progress by holding a philosophy rooted in unbearability attitudes towards the work that you need to put into making and sustaining therapeutic gains. In this case, you need to identify, examine and change these self-defeating attitudes in thought and especially in deed.

704. What you resist usually persists. So, identify and deal with the factors related to your resistance.

705. Learn the difference between a lapse and a relapse. A lapse is a brief, non-significant return to a problem state, while a relapse is a more enduring, significant return to a problem state.

706. View lapses in progress as part of the process of therapeutic change and as opportunities to use your flexible and non-extreme thinking and constructive behaviour, not as signs that you will inevitably relapse.

707. Learn relapse prevention. This involves you identifying and dealing with situations in which you are likely to disturb yourself, rehearsing your flexible and non-extreme attitudes while imagining facing these situations, and then applying these attitudes in the situations themselves.

708. You may disturb yourself about the prospect of a relapse. In this case, assume the worst. Assume that you will relapse and strive to think in a flexible and non-extreme way about it. If you do this successfully, you will both undisturb yourself about this possibility and you will work steadily and unanxiously on relapse prevention.

709. Identify your vulnerabilities to self-disturbance and work steadily and sensibly on these issues in order to decrease these vulnerabilities.

29

On Good Mental Health

710. To think positively about a negative situation is foolish. To think negatively and rigidly about that situation is unhealthy. To think negatively and flexibly about the same situation is wise and healthy.

711. People are frequently preoccupied with knowing that what they experience is normal. They are not so concerned with knowing that their experience is healthy. For normal does not necessarily mean healthy.

712. If you are in two minds, follow the healthy one.

713. To reach the ceiling of good mental health admit that you have flaws.

714. The person who said, 'When you assume, you make an ASS of U and ME' was wrong. It is human to make assumptions. The trick is to treat your assumptions as hypotheses about reality which need to be checked against reality, rather than as unquestionable facts.

715. Think about your problems when you can do something about them. Otherwise, you will remind yourself of your helplessness.

716. Reaching out to others when you could do with help is a strength, not a sign of weakness.

717. Refusing to ask for help when you could do with it is a sign of weakness, not a sign of strength. It shows that you consider yourself to be a weak person if you ask for help.

718. The mind may in many respects rule your body, but if you don't look after your body, your mind may end up ruling a ruin.

719. If you think that enjoying yourself is a waste of time, then take a long, hard look at your life values.

720. Do you feel overwhelmed? Then you probably take on too much in life. It may be useful to ask yourself how, since you are not enjoying the one life that you do have, you are going to enjoy the two (or three) that you are trying to live at the same time.

721. Get yourself a vitally absorbing interest and pursue it actively, but not obsessively. You'll be happier in the long run if you do.

722. If you haven't had at least three good laughs on a particular day, watch a Marx Brothers film (or whatever you find funny) before you go to bed.

723. Spend some time at the end of the day reviewing what you did well that day. If you cannot write down at least ten things you have an unhealthy attitude towards achievement, which is preventing you from recognising what you do well.

724. There are two mistakes that you can make in a leap year (or any other year). You can leap without looking or look without leaping. The healthy approach is to take care while you look, and then make the leap uncomfortably and accept yourself unconditionally if things don't turn out right.

725. There are times when to follow the maxim: 'when it feels good, do it' is definitely a good idea and there are times when doing so is definitely a bad idea. Thinking of your long-term healthy interests will help you to decide which is which.

726. When people are unhealthily disturbed about an adversity they often want to feel less of that disturbance rather than to feel healthily distressed about the adversity.

727. Healthy distress about an adversity, based as it is on a flexible and non-extreme attitude towards that adversity, helps you to change the adversity if it can be changed or to adjust to it constructively if it cannot be changed.

728. Unhealthy disturbance about an adversity, based as it is on a rigid and extreme attitude towards that adversity, interferes with your attempts to change the adversity if it can be changed and with your ability to ad-just to it constructively if it cannot be changed.

729. A person who is mentally healthy wants much and needs very little.

730. Strength is not the absence of weakness. It is how you deal with the weakness.

731. Strive to achieve a balance between your short-term goals and your longer-term goals. If you overly focus on your long-term goals, your life may well be devoid of fun; and if you overly focus on your short-term goals, you may experience little meaning and purpose in your life and mainly experience only temporary satisfaction or pleasure.

732. To maximise your happiness, start with self-interest. Use healthy attitudes to put yourself first, guiltlessly and shamelessly, while holding others a close second (not a distant second). Doing so does not mean that you must put yourself first all the time or that you do not sometimes make sacrifices for others. Do hold yourself responsible for your happiness. You are the best person to choose your life's direction and are most capable of having the required motivation to do what it takes to achieve your personal happiness goals.

733. It is in your best interest to remain interested in the well-being of others and the preservation of your environment. Since you live in a community, strive to live morally and help to protect the rights of others. See that their thriving and yours are interrelated in so far as if they do not have the opportunity to

thrive in life, they may undermine your happiness. Do hold them responsible for helping themselves. Help to preserve the environment as you are part of a larger ecosystem where resources are shared. Your health and the health of others are interrelated.

734. You are the individual best suited to direct your life. Reflect on what you want. Live your life to enjoy yourself and not prove yourself. Avoid devoting your precious time to working towards the goals others have for you and living according to their standards. Consult with experts but in the end, make your own decisions. See that much of your happiness will be derived from time spent striving towards your freely selected goals and values.

735. Expect sometimes to be obstructed by others and the circumstances of life. Unconditionally accept others but work to counter their obstruction ethically. Unconditionally accept life and the challenges of life. See it as hard but not too hard to work against adversity. See that you disturb yourself when life and others obstruct you. See that you anger yourself, depress yourself, and shame yourself. Choose not to disturb yourself when blocked and then engage in creative problem-solving to address adversity. Consistently change what you can change and accept what you cannot. Choose to have some degree of happiness despite whatever hardship you may encounter.

736. Have a vitally absorbing interest or interests in life. Consider intimacy with one or a few chosen individuals. Have a mission in life. When you accomplish one mission, replace it with another. Structure much of your time and devote most of your energy to your mission and to those who are most important to you.

737. Strive to think scientifically. Look for evidence to support your thoughts and hypotheses. Do not adhere to dogma. Regulate your emotions and behaviours through thinking scientifically even when doing so is difficult due to strong emotional urges and when the stakes are high. Use logic and science but recognise life is an art, not a science. Be capable of acting despite not knowing

how things will evolve. Learn from your mistakes and strive to make different mistakes in the future.

738. Unconditionally accept yourself and others with your and theirs good and bad parts. Work on changing those parts of you that undermine your goals. Acknowledge those undesirable characteristics you possess and the self-defeating behaviours that reflect those characteristics. Acknowledge your aliveness and see that you cannot measure your human value based on your traits and deeds. Keep a healthy desire for social approval without becoming reliant on it for your emotional well-being. Acknowledge you cannot change or control others, but you can change and control yourself, and your reactions to what they do, say, and think of you. Encourage others to adopt unconditional self-acceptance and unconditional other-acceptance. Take responsibility for your misbehaviour and do not use unconditional self-acceptance to abdicate responsibility for the impact of that behaviour. Firmly keep in mind that both you and others are fallible humans.

739. See that life involves probability, uncertainty, and risk. Learn to take calculated risks, not impulsive, poorly thought through risks. Hold healthy attitudes towards the possibility of failure when taking calculated risks. Avoid demanding a guarantee before making and sustaining the necessary effort to achieve your goals. Hold fast to your unconditional self-acceptance when the evidence becomes apparent you have failed.

740. Strive to have a healthy balance between immediate pleasure, intermediate satisfaction, and long-term happiness. Take into account the probability associated with the amount of life that you have to live. Work to maximise joy and meaning over the long run while minimising pain. Live for today, tomorrow, and the longer-term future. Keep track of time.

741. See that utopias and perfection do not, in all probability, exist. Acknowledge that all people are fallible humans. Avoid perfectionism. Work to do better and make things better but have a realistic attitude that better never equals perfect. Strive to feel better but accept that you are probably incapable of achieving a

completely joyful and pain-free existence. Accept that as you address one adversity, another will soon follow. Despite life's never-ending stream of challenges, see that you can have some degree of happiness despite the ongoing presence of adversity or deprivation.

742. Maintain a healthy sense of humour. Take yourself, others and life seriously, but not too seriously.

743. Accept the prospect of your death, the death of loved ones, and the process of dying. Appreciate that death will occur, with its hour being the only unknown. Strive to use time wisely, have prioritised goals to lead a meaningful and satisfying life. Do things while time permits. Avoid procrastination. Adopt healthy attitudes to experience healthy negative emotions towards your death and the process of dying. Strive to die with unconditional self-acceptance and unconditional other-acceptance.

30

Miscellaneous

744. When you say that you can't do something, do you mean:

    (a) that you are literally unable to do it,
    (b) that you are able to do it, but you don't want to, or
    (c) that you have the ability to do it but not the skills?

'Can't' applies only to the first scenario, not the other two.

745. When people tell you to 'pull yourself together' they're treating you as if you were a pair of curtains.

746. It is important to distinguish between mood-driven and goal-driven behaviour.

747. Laws may avenge bad behaviour, but cannot prevent it.

748. What you learn determines your behaviour far more than what you are taught.

749. Money won't make you happy, but I'd rather be rich and miserable than poor and miserable.

750. People who tell you that you can do anything you want are giving you dangerous advice if you want to fly as if you were a bird.

751. Be wary of organisations that that say that they have an award for putting people first. Sometimes, these organisations are likely to put awards before people.

752. If you find it difficult to accept compliments, realise that in doing so you are negating the feelings of those who compliment you.

753. From one perspective, if you find it difficult to accept compliments, you can be said to be arrogant. Thus, when you respond to a compliment by saying something like, 'No, it was nothing, really,' you are implying that you are so great that what you are complimented for is commonplace for you.

754. From another perspective, of course, if you find it difficult to accept compliments then you believe that you do not deserve to be complemented.

755. Notice what someone does well and compliment them.

756. Notice what you do well and compliment yourself.

757. Be very sceptical of therapists who comment publicly on the lives of famous people. If they have seen such people for counselling, then they are acting unethically, and if they don't know them personally, then they are speaking from ignorance.

758. People in the mental health field often don't take lunch hours. Then, they have the audacity to run stress management classes.

759. Oversensitivity is often sensitivity plus disturbance.

760. You are more likely to value something that you want if you are made to wait for it than if you have ready access to it.

761. I once heard this on the radio: 'If my father, a Holocaust survivor, could face life with humour and optimism despite what he went through, then I can cope with what life throws at me.' This shows the importance of role models in helping us deal healthily with life's adversities.

762. If you fear being caught with your trousers down, remember that you can always pull them up.

763. In my view, it is disingenuous to embrace fully an experience that you would rather not have.

764. Develop the 'Lionel' attitude. This involves you recognising that life is messy.

765. You can help someone by reminding them that, in all probability, they have in the past dealt effectively with the adversity with which they struggling. They can then implement their own resources in dealing productively with the current adversity.

766. What do want your legacy to be? Let your answer guide your behaviour in the present.

767. Do something kind for someone every day.

768. Do something kind for yourself every day.

769. Memorable phrases will inspire you, but what is memorable is highly individualistic.

770. Moderation is good…. in moderation.

771. Some people say that nothing is permanent except change. Therefore, something is permanent.

772. Don't try to help someone who is not prepared to help themself.

773. If you think that you will get away with something, then you are more likely to do it than if you think that you won't get away with it.

774. My mother used to tell me if you don't ask, you don't get. However, while asking increases the chances of getting, it does not guarantee it.

775. One of the most unfathomable things in my life is why I resonated so strongly in 1965 to the music of Junior Walker and the All Stars and over 60 years later I'm still an avid fan.

776. So, I've stopped trying to fathom it out and now just accept it. If there are things in your life that you don't understand that are similar to this, glory in the wonder of the unfathomable.

777. What is comfortable and normal is not necessarily healthy.

778. Universe is spelt u-n-i-v-e-r-s-e, not y-o-u-n-i-v-e-r-s-e.

779. Knowledge won't set you free. But the application of knowledge may.

780. Being adult means being able to maintain the sense of adultness in the face of being treated like a child.

781. It's not too late to start a new history.

782. Sometimes a person's goals are a reflection of their problem and not the solution to the problem.

783. Lids are for jars, not feelings.

784. Don't give other people advice that you are not prepared to take yourself.

785. Do not search for happiness. Rather, commit yourself to pursuing something that is personally meaningful to you, and you might find happiness along the way.

786. Happiness comes more from striving to achieve a valued goal than from actually achieving it.

787. Get the best out of yourself rather than the self of anyone else.

788. Consider applying the 'baseball rule' to life. When you do something three times and it doesn't work it is time to 'strike out' and use a different approach.

789. People often complain about the simplicity of the ideas expressed in this book. They are simple, but they are difficult to apply. Simple does not mean easy.

790. The quotes in this book will flower if you plant them in your mind and water them with action.

791. Compile and review a quote book of your own containing maxims that you find particularly helpful and inspiring.

31

'Little Gems' from Therapy Demonstrations

792. The rigid attitude leads you to focus on what you didn't do... and edits out what you did do.

793. It's not all a question of self-belief; it's which self you want to believe.

794. Go after things because they are valuable in themselves rather than because of their signal value of how much worth you have to yourself and others as a person.

795. You can take the horror out of badness, but not the badness out of badness.

796. Your task is to take those new attitudes and, do what Albert Ellis used to say, practise, practise, practise.

797. Imagine that you have an illness, and you have to have a complicated operation, but you've got very good private health insurance, so you get to choose your surgeon. Now, it's top of the range insurance, so they give you a choice of surgeons and they're all equally skilful, but they have a different attitude. So, which surgeon would you choose based on their attitude given the fact they're equally skilful? Surgeon 1 comes in and says, 'OK, I guarantee that nothing will go wrong. I'm completely and utterly convinced that this will go well, and I'm so convinced that at some point during the operation I might close my eyes, but don't worry, nothing will go wrong.' Surgeon 2 comes in and says, 'Oh my God, you could die. That would be awful. That would be awful. Oh my God. I couldn't bear it. I can't think about

it. It's terrible.' Surgeon 3 comes in and says, 'Look, this is a complicated situation. You could die. That would be a tragedy, but I'm not turning that into a horror. I'm going to do all the best I can and I'm going to concentrate because I'm not turning a tragedy into a horror.' Which surgeon do you want to do your operation?

798. You're like the hare in 'The Hare and the Tortoise': you wait for the big step to occur and you lie down until it occurs, whereas the tortoise is constantly on the move, taking it step by step and will pass you by.

799. You can feed that belief [I can't do it] – if you want to strengthen that belief, then don't do it and procrastinate, that will do it – or you can actually weaken the belief by acting against it.

800. Accept grim reality when the reality is grim.

801. It's what I call the anti-Magnus Magnusson philosophy: I've started but I don't have to finish.

802. When you say, 'I deserve to get what I want and deserve not to get what I don't want,' your choice is (1) 'It has to be the way I want it to be,' or (2) 'Sadly, it doesn't have to be the way I want it to be.' Which attitude is going to be healthiest for you: it has to be or it doesn't have to be?

803. You're not a poor person – you're a non-poor person who's in a poor situation.

804. So, Dryden's Invitation Technique goes like this. 'I think you're worthless and I invite you to define yourself the same way: that you are worthless.' …when wedding invitations were sent out, they would have RSVP and it would say something like: 'Thank you very much for the invitation and I accept or I decline.' So, '…thank you very much for the invitation for me to define myself as worthless. I accept or I decline.'

805. I think that's a great phrase: 'I'm going to allow myself not to know.'

806. We have met the 'it' and 'it' is you.

807. What you said is perfectly logical. But you've got to act on that so it becomes psychological.

808. So, the issue is not that voice, that demanding voice, what Steve Hayes calls The Dictator.... It's the choices that you make after that voice and the feelings that it engenders. How you respond to that voice.

809. You're going to feed your healthy voice with action, not your unhealthy voice with fighting.

810. If any baby has that attitude, 'I have to know that I can walk before I walk,' what will happen to the baby? He or she will never walk.

811. Saying something stupid doesn't make you stupid unless you define yourself as stupid.

812. The best way to becoming convinced of healthy, flexible and non-extreme attitudes is to recognise that we have a light conviction in them at the beginning, but that we'll strengthen that conviction through action rather than waiting for the conviction to come first and then act.

813. Anxiety is not an impediment to action.

814. So, what you might be doing... is that you are contributing to her hurt feelings, but are you causing them?

815. It's OK to feel bad about doing it, because the badness is in the doing it, not in the you for doing it. There's a difference between, 'It's bad,' and 'I'm bad.'

816. Go forth and be flexible, rather than go forth and be rigid.

817. I'm not asking you to try. People, when they say 'try', as Yoda said in *Star Wars*, 'Do or do not, there is no try.' So, would you like to do or not do?

818. Feeling-based motivation is where you need to feel motivated in order to do it. And, if you don't feel it, you won't do it.' Reason-based motivation is where you do something because there's a reason to do it.

819. Your way of grieving is your way of grieving. You both feel sad at the loss and you're able to get on with life. It's not either/or. It's both/and. You have your unique way, my mother had her unique way, your husband has his unique way, I have my unique way. Who is to say which is the best way? *It's the best way for us.*

820. Albert Ellis, my mentor, once had this list of irrational ideas, one of which was: 'There must be a key that I can find to solve the problem, and I have to find it.

821. I don't need to go back and check, because that's practising my problem and not practising the solution.

822. Albert Ellis says that human beings have two parts of ourselves: an irrational part and a rational part. In the heat of the moment, the irrational part's going to come up. That's not the problem. It's how you respond to it.

823. Years ago, there was a very old programme on British television. It was about medical operations, and it was called *Your Life in Their Hands*. Your solution is *My Worth in My Hands*, not *My Worth in His Hands*.

824. Let's suppose somebody knocks on your door. You go and answer it and you look and no one's there. Then you go back, and they knock again. After about three or four knocks, you're saying, 'Well, I'm still hearing the knock, I'm aware of it, but I'm not going to engage with it.'

825. How can we manage this relationship? It's like you're on a boat. Sometimes other people come and visit the boat, but you're both bringing your strengths and weaknesses to the journey. And there are going to be storms. And some of the time you're going to work together in looking at the storms, sometimes you're going to have to go into your own cabin and recover. But the boat hasn't sunk yet, and I'm not hearing anything that says the boat is sinking. Now, what you're doing is you're saying, 'Oh look, there's another ship over there. I wonder who's on that ship.' That's your tendency. I think that's your way of protecting yourself.

826. It's like an army has got active soldiers and they've got soldiers in reserve. Your active soldiers are responding to a struggle and difficulty with developing self-compassion and self-validation in the face of lack of validation from others. Your reserve soldiers are saying, 'OK, if needed, we're up for a fight. We're in reserve.'

827. Because their behaviour is guided by what was going on in their head and not what was going on in your head.

828. We all have our nature, but we're not a slave to our nature. We're only a slave to our nature if we think we can't change it.

829. In other words, let's put it this way, you have a passport, and you stamp it. On that stamp it says, 'I validate myself. I'm worthwhile because I'm alive, I'm human,' and then you hand your passport to her. She can either stamp it and say, 'I validate you because of what you've been doing under these circumstances,' or not. And, when she hands it back to you and hasn't validated it, your stamp is still there.

830. By giving her the right to be wrong, she doesn't have the upper hand; she's just getting it wrong.

831. You can start to overcome a history of suppression with struggling towards expression.

832. Ask yourself, 'Am I going to do what I don't want to do right now in order to have what I want?'

833. I often say, in going into the past with procrastination, you're procrastinating on dealing with the procrastination in the present.

834. You are not the way you are being treated.

835. I used to be indecisive but now I'm not too sure.

836. It's a bit like you take a train: the first station is rigidity, but you don't have to get off the train. You can say, 'OK, that's the first stop. I'm staying on the train and the next stop is flexibility.'

837. It's whether you struggle and stop or you struggle and move on. And you've been struggling and moving on. And you've got what I call struggle strength: you struggle but you gain strength from the struggle.

838. They don't have more worth unless I choose to give it to them and to take it away from myself.

Postscript

If you've enjoyed this book, tell your friends. If you haven't, tell me. Oh, you can also tell me that you've enjoyed it if you want to. My email address is windy@windydryden.com

Index

ABC Framework 9–12
absence 78, 104, 141
absolute shoulds 10, 12, 13
abstinence 104
abuse 15
acceptance attitudes 11, 30–8
achievement 104, 140
action paralysis 16
active caring 16
acute discomfort 26
addiction 103
adult children 118
adversity 9, 10, 12, 18, 19, 23–5, 28, 29,
    33, 39–42, 51, 53, 54, 78, 82, 107,
    119, 126, 13–7, 135, 140–2, 144, 147
advice 7, 121, 143, 148
aggression 72
aid workers 56–7
alcohol 17, 104
always 22
anger 23, 30, 40, 41, 72–8, 80, 142
anti-shame attitude 62
anxiety 12, 14, 23, 27, 40, 41, 43–50, 60,
    62, 76, 98, 138, 152
anxiety-related intrusive thought 50
appreciate yourself 37
approval 15, 110, 143
Aronin, Georgie 8
arrogance 146
assertion 115–16
assumptions 139
attack 58, 72, 74, 76
attention 15, 50, 109, 114
attraction 84, 85
authority 123
autonomous depression 51–3
autonomous zone 51
autonomy 51
avoidance 45, 93
awfulising attitudes 10, 27–9, 133

bad–awful fallacy 29
badness 29, 37, 48, 66, 119, 150, 152

'baseball rule' 149
basic attitudes 9
bearability attitudes 11, 23–6
behaviour 37, 38, 56, 62, 63, 66, 74, 75,
    80, 81, 83, 99, 106, 108-11, 113,
    115, 131–3, 137, 143, 145, 147, 154
behavioural change 124
behavioural consequences 9
being human 81, 96, 117, 119–21
belief 20, 150, 151
best friend 31, 37
best interests 100, 118, 134, 135
biological parents 118
black-and-white thinking 16
boring, being 36
boundaries 116
brain and world 9

calmness 45
Canute, King 77
caring 16
certainty 17, 19, 39, 47, 85, 86, 98, 99
change 9, 13, 25, 34, 37–40, 74, 99, 104,
    109, 110, 112, 113, 116, 122, 124–
    37, 141–3, 147, 154
children 66, 118, 148
chronic discomfort 26
cigarettes, stop buying 103
cognitive reasoning 122
committed action 128
communication 79
comparisons 32
compassion 37, 60, 154
complacency 37, 132
complaining 115
complex, unratable, unique, fallible
    human being 11, 34, 61
complexity 17, 33, 34
compliments 146
concentration camps 119
concern 40, 41, 44, 45, 47, 50, 60–2, 85
condemnation 31, 45, 66, 75
conditional acceptance attitude 33
conditional should 13

157

confidence 47, 129
confusion 25
consequences 9, 11, 44, 45, 53, 74, 116
constructive action 48, 75, 104, 128, 130, 132
constructive interests 67
continuum 47
control 16, 18, 37, 46–8, 61, 62, 75, 76, 98, 106–7, 143
coping resources 47
courage 48
creative problem-solving 142
critical thinking 121–3

Dali, Salvador 95
danger 15, 17, 91, 128, 145
death 144
de-awfulising 133
decision-making 97–9
defence 76
demands 18, 20, 98, 113, 116
demonstrations, therapy 7, 9, 150–5
denigration 89, 90
depression 27, 30, 41, 51–7
depression-free sadness 53
deprivation 14, 45, 50, 88, 89, 91, 144
desire-ought fallacy 18
desires 11, 17, 18, 21, 32, 88, 89, 90, 92, 101, 112, 122, 143
despair 55
desperation 46
detachment 113
devaluation attitudes 10, 30–8
Dictator, The 152
difficulty 129, 133, 154
disappointment 40, 59, 60
disapproval 59, 60
discipline 100, 103–5
discomfort 25, 26, 93, 100, 103, 133
discomfort anxiety (DA) 43
distraction 45, 127
distress 10, 140, 141
disturbance 9, 10, 12, 13, 15, 17, 34, 35, 49, 55, 61, 76, 98, 103, 106, 107, 112–14, 119, 126, 127, 132, 135, 137, 138, 140–2, 146
  psychological 39–42
dogmatism 14, 15, 21
domination 112
doubts, reservations or objections (DROs) 39, 83, 98, 99, 130

drinking 103
Dryden, Windy 7, 8
Dryden's Invitation Technique 151
duration 136
dying 97, 144
dysfunction 9

early intervention 132
eating 103
ego anxiety (EA) 43
ego-defensive anger 76
elimination 40
Ellis, Albert 150, 153
emotional consequences 9
emotional fragility 19
emotional growth 15
emotional insight 124, 125, 133
emotional problems 39, 40, 61, 109, 117, 127
emotional reasoning 122
empirical should 13
enemies 75, 91, 134
enjoyment 13, 86, 88–91, 140, 142, 156
environment 52, 54, 104, 141, 142
envy 30, 40, 41, 87, 88–92
Epictetus 9
errors 30, 33, 71, 95, 96
evil 29, 119
exaggeration 44, 46, 84, 85
exclusion 61
experience 11, 26, 28, 31, 33, 36, 37, 45–7, 51–3, 55, 60, 65, 75, 76, 86, 94, 103, 107, 119, 130, 131, 133, 136, 139, 141, 144, 147
experts 121, 142
expressing anger 76
extreme attitudes 9, 10. 12, 13, 19, 21, 39, 41, 43–5, 51, 52, 55, 58, 63, 68, 72, 79, 83, 86, 88, 90, 113, 126, 135–7

failure 51, 53–5, 94, 100, 116, 117, 134, 143
fallibility 35, 36, 38, 44, 54, 59, 64, 65, 91, 94, 96, 121, 143
falsehood 121, 123
FAT 103
fear 32, 49, 61, 76, 95, 100, 147
  of flying 48
feedback 32, 94
feeling-based motivation 102, 153

feeling better 127
feelings 13, 20, 42, 44, 46, 49, 52, 54–6,
    60, 63–6, 74, 76, 81, 85, 86, 90, 91,
    93, 103, 113, 116, 122, 126, 128,
    146, 148, 152
    hurt 63
financial worth 31
flexible attitudes 9–11, 12–22, 40, 44, 46,
    49, 51, 59, 61, 64, 67, 69, 75, 77, 80,
    84, 86, 89, 107, 111, 114, 116, 126,
    128, 130, 133–9, 141, 152, 153, 155
fool 31
foolishness 31, 139
forgetting 55, 87
forgiveness 63, 64
foundations 36, 37, 103, 113
Frankl, Viktor 119
freedom 14, 85, 120
frequency 81, 136
friends 8, 31, 37, 122, 133, 134, 156
frustration 72, 73
frustration tolerance 104

game of cards 106
Gandhi, Mahatma 75
getting better 127, 129
global rating 11, 30, 33, 34
global self-rating 31
goal-driven behaviour 145
goals 10, 11, 41, 51, 61, 72, 73, 81, 82, 98,
    103, 104, 127, 132, 134, 135, 141–5,
    148, 149
going against the grain 130
good enough 36
good mental health 139–44
graces 77
grieving 153
grim reality 109, 151
guarantees 46
guilt 16, 30, 40, 41, 60–2, 63–7, 69, 71,
    141
guilt-free remorse 40, 64–6

half-hearted action 128
happiness 23, 24, 141–4, 149
hard work 127, 130
harm 18, 60, 63, 64, 76, 77
    reduction 131
Hayes, Steve 152

healthy anger 40, 73–5, 77, 78
healthy attitudes 11, 19, 128, 134, 141,
    143, 144
healthy boundaries 116
healthy emotions 40
healthy envy 40, 89, 90
healthy goals 10, 11
healthy jealousy 40, 84–6
healthy negative emotions 40, 144
healthy regret 40, 69, 70, 71
healthy relationship 111, 112
healthy response 19, 32, 81
healthy self-control 37, 107
heart, broken 107
hell 17, 61
help 7, 10, 11, 15, 19, 35, 41, 42, 45, 47,
    49, 50, 53, 54, 56, 57, 60, 65–7, 71,
    81, 82, 86, 93, 102–4, 106, 108, 110,
    112, 113, 117, 120, 129, 131–5, 139–
    41, 147–9
helplessness 53, 139
honesty 115
honour their commitments 110
hope 54, 70
hopelessness 53
horror 28, 29, 46, 48, 112, 133, 150, 155
human, being 81, 96, 117, 119–21
humanity 120
humour 144
hurt 30, 41, 60, 76, 79–82, 107
    feelings 63, 64, 66, 152
hurt-free sorrow 40, 82
hypotheses 139, 142

ideal shoulds 13
identity 34, 62
ignorance 120, 146
illness 47, 150
illogicality 9, 12, 23, 27, 30
imagination 135
immediate pleasure 143
immunity 15, 20, 54, 56, 119
imperative 17
imperfections 110
impress, need to 57
improvement 7, 11, 33, 135, 136
impulsiveness 75, 97, 98, 143
inadequacy 31
indecisiveness 97–8, 155
indifference 29

inefficiency 12, 23, 27, 30
inferences 39, 42–4, 51, 53, 58, 59, 63, 64,
    68, 69, 72, 73, 79, 80, 83, 84, 88, 89,
    133
infidelity 84–6
influence 39, 106, 109, 110, 117
injury 39
injustice 56, 75
inner tension 11
insecurity 86
inspiration 100, 119
intellectual insight 124, 133
intensity 132, 136
interesting, being 36
interfering radio stations 40
intermediate satisfaction 143
interpersonal relationships 10
intervention 132
intimacy 142
intrusive thoughts 21
is–ought fallacy 18
isolation 58

jealousy 30, 40, 41, 83–7,
job rejections 55
journey, make the 124–5
joy 143
judgements 33, 49, 98, 119
Junior Walker and the All Stars 148
justice 56, 78

kindness 108, 147
King Jr, Martin Luther 75
knowledge 133, 148

labels 35, 36
lapses 137
laziness 104
learning 65, 71, 120, 129, 131
    difficulties 135
life values 140
'Lionel' attitude 147
listening 19, 40, 108–10, 114, 121, 134
lists 104
'little gems' from therapy demonstrations
    150–5
logic 142
logical fallacies 18
long-term goals 141
long-term happiness 143

long-term interests 134
losers 36
loss 36, 51–5, 84, 98, 99, 153
    of control 16, 46
lovable 31, 36
love 20, 36, 49, 57, 66, 85, 111, 117
loved ones 111, 113, 144

making a fool of yourself 31
malice 73, 74
Marx Brothers 140
maturity 121
Matweychuk, Walter 7, 8
Maultsby, Maxie C. 96
maxims 7, 122, 149
meaning 124, 141, 143, 144, 149
memorable phrases 147
mental fragility 19
mental health, good 139–44
meta-emotional problem 40
mind 17, 18, 20, 21, 89, 95, 98, 109, 112,
    116, 121, 133, 140, 149
miscellaneous 'little gems' 145–9
misery 57
misfortune 20
missions 142
mistakes 17, 66, 71, 95–7, 120, 140, 143
misunderstanding 77
mitigating factors 63, 65
moderation 147
money 31, 145
mood, getting into 100
mood-driven behaviour 145
motivation 12, 18, 22, 24, 27, 28, 30, 33,
    44, 60, 90, 101, 102, 141, 153
mourning 54
Mozart, W. A. 14

narcissism 50
negative life events 15
negative thinking 17
negativity 21, 59
neglect 14, 66, 67
never 22
nominated issues 7
non-anxious concern 40, 41, 44, 45, 50
non-awfulising attitudes 11, 27–9
non-depressed sadness 40, 55
non-extreme attitudes 9, 19, 21, 44, 86,
    128, 133, 135–7, 152
non-foolish act 31

non-judgemental attitude 119
non-poor person 82
non-smoking 103

obnoxious behaviour 115
obstacles 15, 91, 115
OCD 40
opinions 31, 113
optimism 147
organisations 145
other-pity 52, 57
overgeneralisations 21
oversensitivity 146
overvaluation 31
oxygenate healthy attitudes 128

pain 53, 143
painful feelings/issues 46, 49, 93, 127
panic 46, 62
parents 66, 117–18
part–whole fallacy 31
partner, problems with 83–6, 113
passing tests 19, 28
passive caring 16
past 69–71, 80, 81, 97, 147, 155
   conditions 38
   thinking about 71
pedestals 121
perception 15
perfectionism 95–6, 143
permanence 147
persistence 75, 104, 115, 126, 127, 134,
   137
personal change 124–38
   programme 126
personal domain 41–4, 51, 53, 58, 59, 72,
   73, 79, 80, 83, 84, 88, 89
personal habits 127
physical health 119
physical well-being 127, 136
pity-based depression 52
plight-based depression 52, 53
plight zone 51
popular songs 20
possession 40, 48, 88–92
practising 20, 76, 132, 150, 153
preferences 28, 116
   strong 21
pressure 133

pride 62, 120
probability 24, 74, 95, 98, 143, 147
problems 10, 16, 31, 34, 35, 39, 40, 46,
   50, 55, 61, 66, 77, 78, 86, 92, 93,
   104, 106, 109, 113, 116–18, 127,
   128, 136, 137, 139, 142, 148, 153
procrastination 100–2, 144, 151, 155
Procrustes 15
productive action 50
productive work 10, 11
progress 128, 137
provocation 77, 78
psychological disturbance 39–42
psychological health 123
psychological problems 50
psychological well-being 127, 136
psychopathy 66
public speaking 49

quiet, keeping 115

Rational Emotive Behaviour Therapy
   (REBT) 7–11, 13, 40, 41
reactions 40, 132, 143
realisation 48
realistic thinking 21
reality 9, 11, 37, 42, 50, 75, 106, 109, 122,
   125, 135, 139, 151
reason-based motivation 102, 153
reassurance 47, 50, 68, 70, 83, 85, 86, 99
rebellion 100
reciprocation 108
recommandatory should 13
refinement 134
reflection 17, 65, 94, 106, 113, 142, 143,
   148
refugees 56
regret 68–71
reinforcements 54
rejection 32, 33, 42, 55, 107
relapse(s) 132, 137–8
   prevention 137
relationship(s) 10, 11, 31, 49, 79–87
   as boat 154
   with others 108–14
relaxation 47
reluctance 37, 44, 55, 60, 65, 74, 81, 86,
   90, 106, 135
resignation 37, 38

resistance 137
respect 74–6, 109, 118
response 9, 12, 16, 19, 32, 55, 74, 78, 81, 83, 126
responsibility 37, 63, 65, 66, 81, 106–7, 141–3
retaliation 74, 84
revenge 73, 74, 78
rhetoric 20, 122
right to be wrong 20
rigid attitudes 9, 10, 12–22, 39–41, 43–6, 49, 51, 52, 55, 58, 61–3, 66–8, 71, 72, 75–7, 79, 82, 86, 88, 90, 97, 98, 108–13, 116, 117, 125, 126, 128–30, 133–7, 139, 141, 150, 153, 155
Robinson, Smokey 29
role models 75, 118, 147
roses of success 134
rule-breaking 78
ruminating 53, 69, 70, 73, 74, 78

sacrifices 141
sadness 40, 53–5, 153
safety 17, 25
safety-seeking behaviours 44, 45, 136
Scout therapy 78
security 48, 86
seeking reassurance 68, 85, 99
self 32
self-abuse 15
self-acceptance 32, 34, 107, 132, 143, 144
self-assertion 74
self-belief 150
self-blame 65
self-care 67
self-compassion 154
self-control 37, 46, 61, 62, 98, 107
self-defeating 58, 88, 101, 137, 143
self-destructive behaviours 52
self-discipline 103–5
self-disturbance 39, 138
self-encouragement 15
self-esteem 34, 35, 37, 43, 58, 72, 73, 76–8, 91
    low 86
self-evaluative attitudes 62
self-help 135
    books 129, 133
self-improvement 33
self-inflicted insult 39
self-interest 87, 141
self-pity 52, 56, 82

self-punishing behaviour 63
self-rejection 32
self-validation 154
selfishness 67
selflessness 67
sensitivity 146
setbacks 125, 136
shame 30, 40, 41, 53, 58–62, 76, 91, 142
shame-free disappointment 40, 59
short-term goals 141
short-term interests 134
shoulds of preference 13
simple ideas 122
sin 38, 66
    of commission 63, 64
    of omission 63, 64
skills 32, 130, 132, 145
smoking 103, 104
social equilibrium 58, 60
social interaction 60
sociotropic depression 52, 53
sociotropic zone 51
solutions 69, 70, 127, 148, 153
sorrow 40, 80–2
speaking up 115–16
special, being 14
spending 103, 104
stammering 35
Star Wars 153
statement of identity 34
stop asking yourself who you are 36
strengths 19, 36, 139, 141, 155
strong feelings 122
strong preferences 21
struggle 25
struggle–unbearable fallacy 25
stupidity 36
success 94, 134
sulking 79
suppression 155

tenacity 104
therapeutic change 136
therapy demonstrations, 'little gems' from 150–5
thinking 10, 16–18, 21, 39, 71, 95,
    about the past 71
    consequences 9, 1
    critical 121–3
thoughtful action 128
threat 17
TLC 20

tortoise and hare 151
Torvill and Dean 95
transgression 73, 74
travel 17
triumph 74
trying 13, 15, 37, 45, 48, 55, 61, 86, 90,
    110, 112, 129, 133, 140, 148

unbearability attitudes 10, 23–6, 137
uncertainty 47, 83, 97–9, 143
unconditional acceptance attitude 33
unconditional self-acceptance (USA) 34,
    107, 132, 143, 144
unconditional self-esteem 35
unconstructive action 75
underestimation 47
undeserved plight 51
undeserving 56, 72–8, 80
unexplained symptoms 47
unfairness 39, 56, 80, 81
unhealthy anger 15, 72
unhealthy anxiety 41
unhealthy depression 41
unhealthy envy 41, 88–92
unhealthy guilt 41
unhealthy hurt 41
unhealthy jealousy 31, 83, 84, 86, 87
unhealthy negative emotions 18, 23, 24,
    27, 28, 30, 33, 41
unhealthy regret 41, 68, 69, 71, 72
unhealthy self-control 37, 107
unhealthy shame 41
unhealthy thinking 39
uniqueness 36, 91
universe 12, 14, 18, 47, 66, 117, 148
unlovable 31, 36
urges 130, 131, 142
usefulness 89
user manuals 108

validation 154
values 19, 98, 132, 140, 142
vigilance 86
violence 75
viruses 14
visual images 84, 85
Voltaire 75
volunteers 7, 8
vulnerability 15, 19, 25, 28, 34, 35, 47,
    112, 138

weaknesses 61, 139, 141, 154
weeds 14
'what if' questions 34, 48, 100
willpower 103
winners 36
withdrawal 45, 55, 93
wonder of the unfathomable 148
won't power 103
world and brain 9
worrying 46, 48, 49, 150
worth 31, 34, 35, 91, 150, 151, 153, 155
worthlessness 31, 34, 43, 76
writing 13, 14, 100
wrong course of action 69
wrongdoing 65, 66
Wuthering Heights 13